The Big E

Everything is Energy:

*Unleashing the Power of
Everyday Wisdom*

PO Box 754, Huntsville, AR 72740

800-935-0045 or 479-738-2348; fax 479-738-2448

www.ozarkmt.com

The Big E

Everything is Energy:

Unleashing the Power of Everyday Wisdom

By **Jarrad Hewett** and **Dee Wallace**

For permission, serialization, condensation, adaptions, or for our catalog of other publications, write to Ozark Mountain Publishing, Inc., P.O. Box 754, Huntsville, AR 72740, ATTN: Permissions Department.

Library of Congress Cataloging-in-Publication Data
Hewett, Jarrad, 1979 -
Wallace, Dee, 1948 -
   The Big E, by Jarrad Hewett and Dee Wallace
How to create anything you want by unleashing the power of your own energy!

1. Creating Reality   2. Energy   3. Metaphysics
I. Hewett, Jarrad, 1979-   II. Wallace, Dee, 1948-   III. Creating Reality
IV. Title

Library of Congress Catalog Card Number: 2011928631

ISBN: 978-1-886940-25-3

Cover Art and Layout: www.noir33.com
Book set in: Cambria
Book Design: Julia Degan

Published by:

OZARK
MOUNTAIN
PUBLISHING
PO Box 754
Huntsville, AR 72740

WWW.OZARKMT.COM
Printed in the United States of America

Dedication

Dedicated with love to all the trailblazers, dreamers, seekers, knowers, doers, and lovers of love. May your lights shine ever bright.

-       Jarrad and Dee

Table of Contents

Introduction

For those of you new to quantum physics – like we were not too long ago – here are some basic scientific (AGHHH!) principals that will help you understand how energy works:

The first thing we need to understand is that everything is energy – from your Aunt Clara's cat to the cabinets in your kitchen.

That sounds kind of strange, but let's look at it this way: all matter – including us – is made up of atoms (protons, neutrons, and electrons) which are all just varying forms of the big E: Energy.

When we can look at everything as just a part of the big E, we begin to see how amazingly connected everything truly is. It's like that old song, "The knee bone's connected to the... something bone" (I never really paid that much attention), only in this song, the thought bone is connected to the belief bone (which is connected to perception, which is connected to direction, all the way down to manifestation). With this understanding, we've begun to look at our world a bit differently. Science is learning that what we focus on is what we create in our lives. So, from a fat butt to a fat wallet, you can literally change energy with your focus.

In other words, when you feel joyful, your E (your Energy) is vibrating with joyful frequencies; you actually *become* a joyful vibration. How cool!

Guess what? It gets even better, because when you're in your joy, you're able to love yourself – and the world – even more, and as you focus on this joy and love, guess what? More is created – and when you can become the experience of love and joy and focus that love and joy into creating what you want, watch out! The Sky is the limit.

The quickest way to create what you want is to be in a high vibration (love/joy) and to consciously focus, direct, and allow the big E to bring it right to you.

More simply, be happy, say what you want, and go have fun!

Here are the basic FUNdamental steps in creating what you want:

- Choose to get off your butt – nice butt though it is – and go get what you want.

Remember, creation is about choice, so choose to choose so we can get on with it.

- Know what the heck it is you want.

If you already know what you don't want, choose the opposite and try that.

- Keep Focused on what you want.

   Eat it, drink it, sleep it, dream it... and don't let the bed-bugs bite.

- Feel good, happy, and excited.

You know what gets you there; go do it!

- Love yourself, and let others love   you.

   Love conquers all. (Go love!)

- Allow.

   Allow everything you're asking for to come to you easily, effortlessly (did you catch that?), and joyously.

- Allow others.

Don't judge. Don't save. Don't manipulate. Like that one guy who used to have a band said, "Let it be."

Now, as you begin reading, you may find yourself saying, "Well, what the heck does that mean?" Look at you, you instant manifestor. Ask, and you receive!

- Vibrations – What you give forth, or emit, through your energy

- Manifestation – The demonstration or materialization of something

- Focus – What you think about, dream about, want, are in fear of – anything that you "look at" consciously or unconsciously

- Create – Anything you bring into existence/into your reality; Love/Jealousy/A New Car/A Great Mate/A Million Dollars

- Energy – All that is – Everything that exists

- Directing Energy ("The Big E") – Energy is everything. You change energy through choice, direction, and action. Like the transformation from water to ice or steam, The Big E responds to your direction with no judgment.

- Perspective – The view of everything in life from the unique vantage point of your own personal experience

- Polarities – Direct Opposites

Ready to see just how much of an amazing creator you are?

You said, "Yes," right?

Whew!

(We were going to start anyway.) ☺

Let's begin by taking a look at all of those wonderful, cool, old clichés we've all grown up hearing, and re-examining them using a brand new understanding: Everything is *energy* – from here on out, known as "The Big E."

Get ready to let go and re-know what you already knew. Ya know?

Turn the page, and let's get started!

The Left Hand Doesn't Know What The Right Hand Is Doing."

What a way to start! This is the perfect metaphor for our conscious and subconscious minds. If only they communicated and worked together a little more.

Let's take a peek into our mind and see just how these two work:

Conscious Mind:

"I want it! I'm going to get it! I'm going to work hard and be responsible and manipulate things so everything goes my way! I can do this if I work hard enough."

Subconscious Mind:

"Be careful! Do you *really* want this? Maybe it's not the best thing for you. Why do you think you can do this, anyway? You've worked hard plenty of times before and never gotten what you want. Ah...what's the use?"

Imagine how much faster we could institute change and manifest our hearts desires if our conscious and subconscious minds worked together in harmony.

Become conscious of what your subconscious mind is focused on by being aware of your thoughts and feelings – those feelings are indicative of your vibrations, and they will serve as a great guidepost to creation.

"Today is the First Day
of the Rest of Your Life."

This is so true... unless you're dead. But if you're dead, you've probably got better things to do than hang around here and read this book (all though, we don't mind).

No matter what you've done in your past, today is a fresh start. Who you were yesterday is not who you are today. How could you be? In creation, "yesterday" might as well be a whole other lifetime, because you can't create today from yesterday. The only place in which you can create is present time – where it's always time for a present!

So many of us create today based on the stories and labels we're still holding onto. We try to define who we are and what we do. We put ourselves in little tiny boxes and file ourselves away under an infinite amount of categories and subtext.

The truth is, we are beings at choice, and when we can choose to say, "I love myself" and truly move into the power of divine love, you and I will have the power to start fresh because divine love is like the ultimate toggle switch – no matter where you are in life, it allows you a clean slate.

From the standpoint of The Big E, we are releasing the story of who we are and we are creating (as opposed to re-creating) who and what we are in this very moment – which is the moment that will shape the next, and the next, etc.

Here, try this on for size: In the presence of love, I release all definitions of self and other. I lovingly embrace that all are one, and I let go of my story. Today, I AM That I AM. Today, I surrender to the moment. Today is the first day of the rest of my life!

"Don't Worry. Be Happy."

This is perhaps one of the simplest, yet most powerful choices in creation (and thanks to Bobby McFerrin, it's also fun to rock out to). The vibration of worry not only causes us to focus on the opposite of what we truly want, but it also causes us to just feel plain gross. In a universe where we create what we focus upon, worry is the result of fear and only serves to keep us small and in lackmall and in lack. We fear there won't be enough money, enough time, enough US. Some of us worry from the opposite approach – "Oh my gosh; it's really happening." This is really the same vibration of fear and mistrust.

When we can be in a vibration of happiness, the message is sent out to the universe that fear is not what we want. We are consciously telling ourselves that we are not victims, but that we are creators. We are choosing to focus our energy on what it is we want, rather than on what it is we don't. And in THIS moment – the moment of now, which is the only moment we create in – choose to be happy.

"How can I choose to be happy when my life is seemingly in chaos?" says someone whose life is seemingly in chaos.

The answer is love. Think of a moment of total happiness. Love yourself enough to feel your way to a happier thought. Reach out into the infinite field of potentials that you are and *know* you are loved. Think of a baby, a sunset, a new car – whatever it is that will elevate your vibration. Carry that vibration of joy, of happiness, of safety, of love, and from that vibration, *know* that whatever you wish to be, you will be. The key here is to remember that now is the moment from which you create all others.

Today is a gift. How will you choose to spend it?

"Shit Happens."

I have a friend who once had a tree fall on her house. Her neighbor came over and, trying to ease her mind, looked at her and exclaimed, "Ya know, shit happens." Without missing a beat, she looked him dead in the eyes and said, "Yeah? Well, I sure wish shit would have happened on *your* house."

"Shit happens" is the ultimate statement of a victim consciousness, and most of us have heard it all our lives. Some of us have even taken it a step further by stating, "Shit happens, and then you die." With this idea, there is an expectation that bad things are going to happen no matter what we do. More importantly, there is an acceptance of this belief that literally serves to continually create random instances of total shit. The belief behind this self-feeding cycle is one of powerlessness: "I am a separate being who is at the mercy of a greater outside force."

What we must realize then, is that in a world of one consciousness, there is no separation. Everything is part of The Big E. There is no such thing as a random occurrence. There is no outside force. Therefore, the only shit that happens is the shit we create.

If something "crappy" comes into your consciousness, turn your frown upside down. Wherever there's shit, there's usually a pony – and who doesn't like ponies?

"That's Just the Way it Is."

"Shit happens" has an ex-wife named "That's just the way it is." They were married for many years, but one day, "that's just the way it is" fell in love with a higher vibration, and that was the end. The relationship between these two was interesting – if not codependent – to say the least. You see, while with Mr. Happens, "That's just the way it is" was constantly re-enforcing his belief, and so, the two went through life constantly dodging trees because Mr. Happens was holding the belief and the expectation that were causing the trees to "randomly" fall.

One day, however, "that's just the way it is" realized that she was her own creator, and that her thoughts created her reality. You see, "Mrs. Is" was giving her creation over to whatever energy she was around, and not claiming her own power. The day she realized that she had been giving her power away, she saw her husband for what he was – just a belief. When she was able to see that, she was able to re-claim her own power and fall in love with herself.

Now, she loves herself, and remains in the knowing that she is always taken care of because *she* is the only one who can create her world – because... that's just the way it is.

"That's The Last Straw."

We've all said it:

"That's it; I'm not going to play this game. I'm mad as hell, and I'm not going to take it anymore!"

Oh, if only that were true. If only we *were* done playing the game.

But alas, most of us LOVE to hold on to grudges. We love to stay in the anger and judgment and *wallow* in our stuff. Our anger keeps us in a place where we're constantly being buried under the weight of more and more straw. In truth, that final straw is really just an opportunity for us to shift our focus and really move on to what we want, and the only way to do that is to learn our lesson and love ourselves enough to let go and move on.

If we can't do that, that last straw won't just break the camel's back – it'll break ours.

"Dare To Dream."

OMG! How sad to think someone actually had to give this direction to another human being. It is the very core of creation.

As the song "Happy Talk" from *South Pacific* states, "You've got to have a dream. If you don't have a dream, how you gonna have a dream come true?"

The Dream is the desire and the seed that eventually grows into the THING!

So, why would anyone dare NOT to dream?

Well, it's safer, for one thing. If we don't dream, we don't risk our dream not coming true. We also get to remain in our "crap" and gain sympathy and camaraderie from our Birds of a Feather Friends who are not daring to dream either. We also get to remain "powerless" over our lives – which is sometimes a whole lot easier (and much more acceptable) than knowing that we are our own creators.

As Maryanne Williamson said, "Our deepest fear is that we are powerful beyond measure." What if we DO create the dream we dared to dream?

Dare to live the life you've always wanted. Like an over-stocked candy store, our dreams are filled with every delicious treat we could ever imagine, and imagining them is the first step in getting a vision for what we want to create. All we have to do is dive in, and dare to dream.

"The Sky Is The Limit."

Literally, there are no boundaries to what we can imagine and create. The Big E is here to give us everything we want, and like a good actor, the Big E follows directions to a T and will *always* deliver the performance we ask for.

The Universe is truly limitless and without judgment. The Big E will give us everything we ask for without thinking we are selfish, unworthy, or even unappreciative – those are all labels spawned from guilt, and the Big E won't give us guilt unless we ASK for it (AKA direct it to match our belief).

Here's the thing about guilt, we usually don't let it in unless someone else has told us we should. Guilt is simply a self-propelling idea. Letting someone convince us that we should feel guilty for going for our dreams doesn't serve us, it serves them. It validates their own belief systems about guilt, which they probably got from somebody else, who got it from somebody else, or society, or through their own fearful thinking.

So open your arms, and let love in. Let abundance in. Follow your joy. Be like a child, and ask for every little thing you want! The Universe is abundant. There is more than enough. All you have to do is ask.

"Let Bygones Be Bygones."

Most of us would like to make bygones – stay gone! Energetically, a stay gone is an oxymoron because if we are focused on something staying gone, we are still focusing on the thing that should be gone – thus bringing more of that thing into our existence.

So, why do we hold on? What kind of ride do we get to take by keeping our focus on the things we don't want? Well, to answer those questions, we have to ask a few more: "Who are we really hurting by holding a grudge anyway? Whose feelings are kept out of joy, and whose focus is kept off of creating happiness?

The answer is: OURS!

Look at it this way:

Holding the junk:

1) Makes *us* unhappy

2) Keeps *us* focused on what we DON'T want (which is more of whatever we're trying to let go of)

3) Keeps *our* vibrations in judgment, anger, revenge, lack, etc.

4) Keeps *us* STUCK.

Whatever nasty things you're lugging around, get rid of it. Let go, and let The Big E start working for you!

If you can choose to say "bye" to all of your baggage, it'll have no choice other than to *be gone*. Turn to that baggage and repeat after me, "Buh-Bye!" It's that easy if you'll let it be.

"The Road to Hell is Paved
With Good Intentions."

Do I need special tires for that?

This one can be kind of confusing – especially if you're under the impression that doing good is, well, good.

If the road to hell is paved with good intentions, what's the road to heaven paved with?

Well, the answer is, "the same thing."

The message here is that wanting to do good isn't enough, and that sometimes trying to do "what's right" or "what's good" can get us in a whole heap of a mess. When someone has a good intention which translates into an action everyone approves of, 'bravo!"

The thing is, what's good for goose's creation may not be good for the ganders.

In other words, someone else's good intentions along with a dollar fifty will buy you a cheap cup of coffee.

There is a fork in this metaphorical road, and the one to h-e-double hockey sticks is the one you take trying to create for someone else. No matter what your intention is, you just can't do it. The only person who can create for them is them.

Take the fork that leads to you. Create the world you want by loving yourself enough to know that you can only create for you. When you can release having to control anyone else, the rest is gravy.

"Cast Not Your Pearls Before Swine."

Why?

'Cause they just don't get it. They don't want to. They can't – they're pigs!

Besides rooting around and pushing the pearls further into the mud, what would a pig do with pearls? They certainly have no worth in a pig's life.

Realize that your positive outlook, your knowledge of vibrations and manifestation, and your lofty ideas are all pearls. Those pearls are lost on anyone whose story and commitment is "I am a victim, and I have no control over all this horrible stuff in my life" or "no matter what I do, nothing is going to change." Those people don't want to get your story of healing and happiness because they have too much invested in their stories of struggle and hardship.

When we cast our pearls before pigs, our pearls get dismissed. We get argued with, doubted, and challenged. Energetically, we're trying to mix with birds of a much different feather.

We have to know that our job is not to fix anyone or anything. Our job is to love ourselves, honor ourselves, respect ourselves, and BE HAPPY.

So if you are asked, share. If you are given an opening, take it.

Otherwise, share your pearls with someone of like energy who can exchange something of value with you – and enjoy the abundance.

"Chance Favors The Prepared Mind."

Chance favors the prepared mind because the prepared mind knows that it is prepared – and it knows that it knows, ya know? Energetically, when we *know* we know, everyone else vibrationally *gets* that we know. Then THEY can know. How awesome is that? What looks like "luck" is actually the Big E going, "Hey, I've got a knower at 5:00 o'clock; let's go there!"

Now, some people can study, learn, and prepare, and never know, while others can do nothing and *already* know.

It's really more about knowing we are enough and that we are loved, creative, and committed than it is about being prepared. Preparation is great for math tests and algebra, because no matter how much I've committed, I still have to know what π means – but I also have to move into the OTHER Knowing – The metaphysical, peaceful knowing. Otherwise, what I know (the data) will be cancelled out by the fear that I don't know, which ultimately results in $-X + X = 0$.

So, be prepared, and *know*. That way, you can let go and be in the flow of allowing.

"The Early Bird Gets The Worm."

I love this saying because to me, it has two meanings. The first describes my thinking for the first fifteen or twenty years of my life: "If you want something, you'd better be willing to work twice as hard as anyone else and do whatever it takes, because there aren't a whole lot of worms out there, and only the people willing to kill themselves and do whatever it takes are going to get a worm."

As I believed, I received. I was a great student. I worked my tail off, and I got the worm... but I was so miserable trying to beat everyone else, that by the time I got the worm, I despised it because of all the sacrificing I'd had to do in order to get it.

So what changed?

Well, it wasn't until I shifted my perspective and started looking at this as an excuse to start drinking tequila before noon that...

No. I kid. That wasn't it.

The real shift came when I began looking at *all* of life as a worm. I began to see life in a bigger context – it wasn't just about taking a test, getting a job, finding a mate, it was about being able to enjoy the experience of *all* of it.

Enjoy my job? Are you crazy?

It all comes down to this: Happiness is a choice. If you choose to be happy, you will be happy. You don't have to physically wake up earlier than anyone else to get your "worm"; you just have to wake up to the joys of life. Once you can do that – worms everywhere!!

"There's More Than One Way to Skin a Cat."

So, let me see if I have this right. The early bird gets the worm. Old dogs can't learn new tricks. And cats get skinned? What did cats ever do to you Mister Guy-Who-Comes-Up-With-Proverbs?

PETA protests and uncomfortable visuals aside, this is really a positive statement. A lot of times we get so set in our ways that we just can't see any other options. What we need is a new perspective so that we can open up to new thoughts and ideas.

Vibrationally, happiness *comes* from being happy. What happens though is that we sometimes limit our definition of happiness.

For example, there was a point in my life where I defined happiness by my ability to make money. I had a wonderful house that was completely paid for, an awesome car that ran, and wonderful friends – but I was so focused on how much money I had in the bank, that none of those things mattered.

The only way to skin my cat was to have a lot of money in the bank. Once I took my focus off of making more money and placed it on appreciating all of the great things and people in my life, I found that I was suddenly much happier (and I made a lot more money). I had realized that happiness wasn't just about money in the bank – that there was more than one way to skin that cat.

This phrase is a reminder not to limit ourselves, but it's also a reminder not to limit the Universe. How many times have you gotten something in a way that you never would have expected? The Energy knows

27

what's up – and it knows ways that we couldn't possibly imagine. So when you can't see a way, chill out. Relax. Kick back, and know that there is more than one way to skin a cat.

"Look Before You Leap."

Can't you just feel the fear?

"What if it's too steep?" "What if I fall?" "What IF I DIE?" "I've got to be sure!"

Unfortunately, we have taken a sound piece of physical advice and accepted it as the life-and-death rule for everything.

This contradicts a very important principle of the Big E.

Energetically, the *less* we fearfully "look" at something – break it down, weigh its advantages and disadvantages, or try and figure out its worth – the better off we are. Sure, looking is good when you're buying a car, but not when you are divinely inspired by an idea. Divine inspiration comes from a place that, oftentimes, our intellect just doesn't understand. Have a little faith!

When we break a divine inspiration down into what makes "sense," we often times don't act on it. That little ego comes in and yells, "Warning. Let me protect you. Don't proceed because you don't know how," or "it doesn't make sense."

Well guess what Mr. Ego? The first airplane "didn't make sense." The first automobile was laughed at! The pet rock made no sense – and sold millions!

So, if you're maneuvering your way through a floor covered in snakes, look DOWN and watch your step, but when it comes to inspiration, ideas, and dreams – LOOK WITHIN. Pull from that place where all possibilities exist and all information is available. Then walk, leap, skip, and jump your way into that divinely gifted glimpse of no limitation – and know that gift is you!

"It Must Be Nice..."

Oh c'mon. I mean, really? When most of us say this, we don't actually *mean* "it must be nice" (whatever "it" is). The vibration behind this statement is more, "Okay. I've tried really hard, and I work all the time, and I have these great dreams, and I think I'm worth getting what I want and – Sigh – It must be nice...getting everything *you* want.

Behind that vibration is the belief that either we can't, or we won't. Even if we can appreciate that someone else has "it," we still feel bad and envious because we don't.

So, you see the mixed messages we're sending out as directions to the Big E? We're telling the Big E, "I want these things" while we're *also* sending the message, "but I'm envious and depressed because someone else has it (ergo sadness and depression become collapsed with having AND wanting)." The Big E, which creates from our direction, just goes, "...Okay??"

Like a child who is told to go to their room without moving a muscle, the Big E simply can't deliver something we want as long as we're also holding negative or opposite vibrations.

So, if we're going to be happy for someone, let's go all the way! Let's invite *all* our vibrations to go "Yee-haw!" "Yippee – he has it" and "Woo-hoo, I'm creating it!" There is enough awesomeness and abundance for everyone. The more yippee and yee-hawin' we do, the more the Big E can bring us what we want.

YEE-HAW!

"There Is Harmony In Disharmony."

Polarities appear to exist in everything: good/bad, up/down, rich/poor, etc. In reality, it's all the same energy. The "polarity" is just an indication of judgment and focus. For example, if I believe in unconditional love, on some level, I must believe in conditional love – otherwise, there would be only love. So it is with harmony and disharmony. By being conscious of the choices we make and of our emotions, we can literally change our perspective and see order in disorder and harmony in disharmony. If we know that everything is energy, we know that no matter what the appearance, there is an inner belief being manifested, and thus everything is always as it should be.

The Big E will bring us whatever we focus on.

If we have disharmony in our lives, we must shift our perspective and focus on harmony. When we can do that, harmony will be created. The tricky part is being aware enough to direct your focus to the positive polarity. That's always what you want: the positive.

We know that we get what we focus on (or think about, or worry about, or are in fear of), so when we are sick, can we focus on being well? Can we focus on wealth and abundance while we joyfully pay off our debt?

Can we choose to feel excited ('cause the Big E *LOVES* feelings) while we tackle our growth opportunities? (Notice we didn't say "problems!")

Focus your energy on what you want, and live the harmonious life of love you deserve!

"Live And Let Live."

Well, where's the ride in *that!*? If I can't fix, save, or judge someone, what am I supposed to do with me? After all, those things are how I define myself in relation to the rest of creation; it's my story!

If our focus is on somebody else, we simply don't have to deal with our own fears, limitations, and responsibilities. What we don't realize though, is that we are looking between the bars of our own self-made prison: limited perspective and judgment. Judging, fixing, and saving are all cages that we put ourselves in to help keep us from having to deal with our own issues.

The Big E is very clear: we only create for ourselves – that goes for all of us. When we allow ourselves to be who we are, AND ALLOW EVERYONE ELSE TO BE WHO THEY ARE, life flows into an acceptance of oneness.

Some of the ways we can climb out of limitation are by allowing everyone to worship the way they need to, define the Big E the way they need to, dress the way they want to, vote the way they want to, etc.

When we live – and let everyone else live – in balance and happiness, co-creation of Peace and Love Is Possible.

"That's A No Brainer."

Whoo-Hoo! Let's hear it for the No-Brainer!

The more we can get out of our brains and into our hearts, the better off we'll be.

As Einstein said, "Imagination is more important than knowledge." We create through our creativity, our passion, and our instinct. The good old brain usually plays the devil's advocate to all of these by pulling us back into "reality."

That's probably why meditation is so big within the New Age Movement. It forces us to become quiet, get out of our "heads," and experience the Universe creatively speaking through our hearts.

This is not to say that the brain has no use, it's just that most of us have it backwards. We tend to lead with our thoughts instead of first checking in with our still, small voice. Instead of leading with the brain, use it to direct the Big E to manifest what the little voice has to say. We can direct the brain to guide our creativity in fabulous ways, but the creative impulse – the little voice, the divine idea – comes from the heart, and it is the heart that truly creates... and that, folks, is a no-brainer.

"An Idle Mind Is The Devil's Playground."

Once again, we see the importance of perspective and how it applies to a situation.

To the mother of a teenager with seemingly no goals and a penchant for laziness, this statement is going to ring incredibly true.

It's like my grandmother used to say, "Give them free time, and they'll be up to no good before you know it."

Let's take a minute and look at this statement from another perspective.

To the Tibetan Monk or the teacher of meditation, an idle mind is THE place to connect with the Big E (you know, "empty your mind, and connect with the universe."). If our minds are always full, it's hard to hear the still small voice that often inspires us and tells us how to get wherever it is we wish to go.

So you see, this phrase rings true either way. The only difference is the belief we *choose* to associate with it. The rewards we reap will also depend on that choice, because our belief in its truth will create that very outcome in our life.

The first truth yields trouble, while the second gives great insight.

Ergo (don't you love big words), perhaps choosing the perspectives that are happy, healthy, joyous, and abundant, aren't so... Poly-Anna.

You can change your mind right now if you CHOOSE, and by changing your mind, you can literally change your life!

So, what choices do you choose to change today?

"If The Cap Fits, Wear It."

In other words, take responsibility for your creation. In understanding the Big E and how we create, this is the most important principle to comprehend.

If it's your cap, wear it. If it's your prejudice, heal it. If it's your fear, let it go. If it's your limiting belief, redefine it.

When you can accept and take responsibility for your life, you will be in a place of authorship. Once you can accept your authorship, you will be free to redefine and re-write whatever subjects in your life you wish to change.

The basic truth that you *must* get is that you – and only you – are the creator of your life. "The buck stops here," as they say. There is an inner reason for every single outer manifestation.

Whenever we point the finger at someone or something else as a cause or excuse for our shortcomings, we are really giving away our creative power. We are literally saying, "Here. I can't do anything about this because of you. Therefore, you create my life, not me; I give up."

If we don't create our own life, we become created upon – whether we're consciously aware of it, or not.

So, if you want to lose weight, find the energetic hat that will create losing weight, and wear it proudly. Go dig out that beret buried in your subconscious, clean it up, and make some money! Take that soured old rain hat and throw it away! Plant that sun bonnet firmly on your head - because let me tell ya, it's gonna be a bright (bright, bright), sunshiny day!

41

"Better Late Than Never."

I think The Big E would agree with this entirely. You know why? Get ready for it... Because there is no time in the reality of all that is. The energy that is here has always – and will always – be right here in the now. Time is a concept that man devised so he could understand the limitless of the universe through limitation.

Why on earth would we do that?

Well, one reason is because it helps us control the world we live in as well as our lives and the lives of others. This false concept of control has created manufactured pressures that we really don't need, i.e.: I've got to, I have to, etc.

The Big E is always expanding and always loving. You can't get it wrong. You can't fail, and you absolutely can't be late in "getting there" when "there" exists forever.

Whenever you get to where you need to be is the perfect time for you to be there. In fact, not *trying* to get there usually gets us there faster – because instead of focusing on "there" we're focusing on here, and "here" is where we create everything.

So, when we choose to be "here," we can't ever be late for "there," because "there" becomes "here" and that's where we already are! Got it?

Just be. As a matter of fact, love being - celebrate being – because my friends, we have arrived!

"Laughter Is The Best Medicine."

We know that when we love ourselves fully – on all levels – the vibrations of what we are asking for and the vibrations of what we are receiving match up easily and effortlessly. We are asking for what we want out of a true desire – a desire we have no real attachment to because we know (mentally, emotionally, and vibrationally) that all is well. We know we are taken care of.

That said, the best thing we can do for ourselves – *ever* – is simply to feel good and love ourselves.

Now, when someone is sick, you can give him or her a pill and they may feel better. Vibrationally, what has happened is, the pill has allowed them to re-establish and re-claim their own creation of wellness. If they have placed their belief in the pill, it will work for them, and their vibration will be raised into health and they will feel better. Now, if you have a headache (or as I like to call them, my sister's kids), aspirin will often make you feel better – whereas the act of physical laughter might actually make your headache worse. In the same vein, laughing when you have a hernia is not really that pleasant. How then, did the expression "laughter is the best medicine" take such a hold in our vernacular?

The vibration of laughter is associated with the vibrations of joy, of love, and of lightness. There is an association with laughter that is the opposite of serious. Laughter is light. Laughter is playful. So, what the phrase is really saying is: Yes, you can give me aspirin for a headache (or a baby sitter), and you can give me a mood stabilizer for depression (or again, a baby sitter), but the best medicine for what ails me is to know that I am not that thing.

Imagine being able to laugh at all of it. Imagine if we knew that we were always loved and protected and that we didn't cease to exist after death – would everything seem quite so serious?

Laughter is a way to shift our focus off of the perceived "seriousness" of life, and in that regard, "laughter is the best medicine."

"You Have To Walk Before You Can Run."

Who says?

Well, I suppose if we started out only knowing how to run, stopping might be a bit of a problem. I mean, it might be difficult to start out EXPLODING into total freedom and then having to learn how to subdue ourselves into "taking it slow" by walking.

Most of us came into this life as cute little bundles who couldn't really do that much except look cute and cry. After a while, we noticed all of this stuff going on, and we started trying to look around. Through this interaction with our environment, we discovered our neck muscles. Next, we started rolling around and crawling. Eventually, hanging out in our own poop while waiting on someone to bring us a cookie got old (mostly because of the poop), and we started wanting to do things for ourselves. We started wanting to move – and we learned how. This is a wonderful illustration of a key concept of creation: Creation is born from the desire to move and the wanting to expand.

When we were little, we had the desire to move. We had the desire to learn how to express our little selves! Most of us fell down time after time, but it didn't matter, because we were babies; we were just learning. We knew we'd get there eventually, and we did.

Wherever we are right now is perfect because from where we are now is arising the desire to create something else – whether that be a better marriage, a new marriage, better health, more money, more time for our families, whatever. Everything we are experiencing now is simply the process of learning to create something new. We're just learning to run. In a way, we're still like little babies. We've just got to remember to know what we want and not let anything stop us. If we get tired of falling down, all we have to do is point and direct. The big E will bring us everything we want, and all we have to do is allow.

"Like Father, Like Son."

"Like father, like son" is one of those fun, old-time phrases used to illustrate similarity or connection – in this case, it's a similarity or connection implicit from birth. It's ultimately been used as a phrase for dis-empowerment or dismissal. If someone comes from a successful family and they are successful, we say "well, like father, like son." If someone is a crook and his father is also a crook, we say "well, like father, like son."

(...I'm sure glad my dad was good looking AND smart!)

The truth is, we are not only "like" the energy we have come from, we *are* that which we have come from. I'm not talking about inheriting the traits we think make us who we are: eye color, skin color, temperament, IQ, height, etc.

I may have gotten my brown eyes from my physical father, but I also got them from my energetic father: Mr. E. I got them from my desire to have the experience I am having right now. You see, according to the Big E, I am the father of my creation and therefore I am the only person and circumstance that can claim the responsibility for what my life has been, has become, or what it may yet be.

In accepting and knowing that I AM the creative force in my own life, I free myself to experience and create my wildest dreams.

"Like Water off a Duck's Back"

When I was a kid, my family lived on a good-sized piece of land that backed up to a large lake. Much to the enjoyment of the ducks that lived in the lake (and the chagrin of my parents, who *clearly* felt the duck's "treasure" was their "trash"), we also had a heated pool. During the fall months, when the air became a little nippy, the ducks would migrate to our pool. To a kid, this was kind of cool. I had the opportunity to go swimming with the ducks. To my parents... well, let's just say that ducks aren't that discriminating when it comes to matters of the digestive tract.

My mom would run out to the pool with her trusty broom– often times with kids in tow, and we would shoo the ducks from the pool. Those of us who didn't have brooms, used a different means of persuasion – splashing, but the thing about the ducks was, no matter how much water we managed to pile onto them, they stayed dry. Occasionally, one would rear up, spread his little duck wings, and ruffle off the water, but they never stayed wet. Think about that – ducks live in water, yet they don't get water logged. They just shake it off and stay dry.

Within the pool of the one consciousness (the Big E), how dry are you? Are other people throwing water on you? Are you throwing water on yourself? If you are, are you getting water logged, or are you just scooting on over to the next heated pool without a care in the world? Nothing is so serious that it needs to wet our feathers and render us incapable of floating. We know that we create everything, so there is really nothing to be afraid of. If we don't like something, all we have to do is shift our focus and create what we do want. We've simply got to take a little energy cue from our floating friends and be more, well... duck-ish. We've got to look at everything that's thrown our way as water. We can drink it in, swim in it, float around, or say "no thank you," shake it off, and move on.

"Many Hands Make Light Work"

Most of us heard this in our youth, and it was usually in reference to helping people do things no one particularly wanted to do. We all know that through pooling our physical effort, we can achieve our goals more quickly. As my roommates from college would be quick to point out, four people can clean a house quicker than one (of course, they'd only say that when it was their turn to clean). Well, shifting the thoughts and energy of the collective consciousness works the same way.

Think of this as a metaphor for the consciousness of light and love. It becomes a much broader concept with a very simple explanation.

Within my own physical being – my physical house that is an expression of my spiritual being – I have many vibrations. The more I can focus on uniting my personal vibration in love, the more I, as an entire expression of all that I am, can experience love. When I am able to shift my consciousness into one of love and abundance, I radiate those vibrations into the Big E, which radiates them back. My knowing serves as a marker for others who are experiencing their desire to experience love and abundance and helps enable them to raise their vibrations as well. The more consciousness we have of light and love, the more that light and love can flourish and expand.

Consciously, when we can experience our self as the love that we are, we are in full allowance and that which we have called forth has no choice other than to be made manifest. When our consciousness is united in the light, ALL works, and it works easily and effortlessly – for our many hands, make light work.

...but it's still your turn to clean the kitchen.

"Never Judge a Book by its Cover"

We all have an idea of how things are supposed to look – an idea of how "good" looks, of how "evil" looks, of how "success" looks, etc. Sometimes, it's those ideas that keep us from receiving whatever it is we've been asking for. One of the best illustrations of this principal is a joke I once heard in church:

It had been raining for days, and a terrible flood had come over the land. The waters rose so high, that one man was forced to climb onto the roof of his house. Climbing up to the roof, the old man asked The Big E to save him.

The waters continued to rise as a man in a rowboat appeared, "Hop in" he shouted to the old man. "No thanks," replied the man on the roof. "I'm waiting on the God. Thanks, though!" As the man in the rowboat went away, the old man, secure in his conviction, once again asked The Big E to save him.

The waters rose higher and higher, and suddenly a speedboat appeared. "Climb in!" shouted a man in the boat. "No thanks," replied the man on the roof. "I'm waiting on The Universe!" So, the man in the speedboat went away. Once again, the old man on the roof directed the Big E to save him.

The waters continued to rise. A helicopter appeared and over the loud speaker the pilot announced he would lower a rope to the man on the roof. "No thanks," replied the man on the roof. "I'm expecting the Big E to save me any minute now." So, the helicopter went away, and once again, the man directed The Energy to save him.

The waters rose higher and higher, and eventually they rose so high that the man on the roof was washed away, and alas, the poor guy drowned.

Upon his arrival to the "other" side, the man marched straight over to The Big E and said, "What was all of that? I asked you to save me. Where were you?" The Big E gave the man a puzzled look, and said "I sent you two boats and a helicopter. Why didn't you get on?"

Oftentimes, we wind up rejecting exactly what we've been asking for because we don't understand the delivery process or we judge the package. We ask The Big E to send us the desires of our hearts, and then we don't get off the couch to answer the doorbell because we don't recognize who is at the door.

Well friends, our job isn't to judge anything. Our job is simply to place our order and sign for its delivery.

"No Pain, No Gain."

Well that sucks.

But oh, we tell ourselves this all the time. Whether we're on crunch number 9,702 at the gym, weathering the storm of a rocky relationship, or we're just generally miserable and using this expression as a means to try and cheer ourselves on, "no pain, no gain," has become a battle cry we use to push ourselves. Well, the reason we're pushing ourselves and struggling to achieve our goals is because we've energetically bought into the notion that pain and gain go hand in hand. We've bought into the idea that in order to make progress, we have to suffer, and as we know, we create what we focus upon.

If we believe we can't have gain without experiencing pain, we won't. With this belief, the vibrations of pain and gain become married in our energetic bodies to the point where every time we send out the vibrations of gain, we are also directing The Big E to bring us pain – and who wants to live with that couple?

In a relationship, it might look like a wonderful relationship where we're both in debt. If we want to lose weight it may look like having to starve ourselves or having to hit the gym extra hard. What we have to do, is separate the idea of pain from the idea of personal expansion and joy.

When our truth can become "through love, gain" everything will come to us in an easy and joyous manner. Those loose ends that we've been trying so desperately to tie up will suddenly take care of themselves because the vibrations of struggle we have been sending out along with our direction for completion will cease to be. Those pounds will fall away not because we are starving ourselves, but because we love ourselves.

On another level, this statement relates perfectly the concept of energetic polarities (I want it/I don't want it). If I believe I have to experience pain in my life to get what I want, I can ultimately experience never getting what I want, because what could be more painful than a life spent always asking and never getting? Another way of looking at this belief in action is to say that when I get what I want, others must suffer.

Love yourself enough to know that you deserve what you want. Know that The Big E is loaded with everything anyone could ever ask for, and there is plenty of everything for everyone. How others choose to create is not your business. Your job is to love it all, and create what *you* want: expansion through love.

"You Can't Make A Silk Purse
Out of a Sow's Ear."

The variation of this little idiom I always heard was, "You can't make peanut butter from poop." Then again, why would you want to? Last time I checked, a poop and jelly sandwich didn't really seem like something I'd like to eat.

It's the same thing as not making a silk purse from a sow's ear. If you were trying to create a cake, you would not go to the grocery store and buy vegetables and steak.

So why do you expect to become successful while holding the vibration of "I am a failure?" You can't create happiness from vibrations of unhappiness. Instead, acknowledge the vibration you are in, and shift your perspective. By changing your perspective, you can change your vibrations. Don't be afraid to find the positive in every situation.

After all, you might not be able to make peanut butter from poop, but you *can* buy some with all the money you'll save on fertilizer.

"There Are No Victims, Only Volunteers."

From "shit happens," to "that's just the way it is," we've looked at the things we tell ourselves to let ourselves off the hook. Now, let's look at the statement that puts the broom of life right back in our hand. "There are no victims, only volunteers."

You mean *I'm* responsible for *all* of this? Yep.

Clean up, *isle me!*

Whatever you are experiencing in your life that you deem "crappy" is your own doo-doo. The good news is that by owning it, you can clean it up. All you have to do is let it go.

No one has the power to create for you, just as you do not have the power to create for anyone else, unless that power is given over. Even then, the power is still ours; we are just allowing someone else to use it. To take responsibility for your life means just that – you are responsible. Some of us have experienced violence in our lives. How do we explain this?

Taking responsibility does not mean taking the blame. If someone punched me, and I received the punch, whether I like it or not, that punch was created by me. I am not blaming myself for being punched, or saying that the person who punched me is off the hook, but I am saying that energetically – whether through pain, anger, doubt, whatever the energy may have been – I was holding enough of something that created its manifestation, and that manifestation came in the form of a punch.

The good news is, once I know this, I'm home. When I can take responsibility for everything – not just the things I call good, and not just the things I call bad, I am vibrationally saying, "You know what? It's all good. I know that I am my creator, and I know that whatever is created is for the best. If I am holding an energy strongly, it will manifest in some way, shape of form as an opportunity for me to either validate my belief or change it. From this manifestation, I will grow and continue to expand on my journey." We are not victims of circumstance; we are volunteers. The choice as to whether we volunteer for our own victimness or choose to own our own creation is up to us.

"We Shall Overcome."

Wow. Just saying it is a downer.

In order to overcome, there must be struggle. There must be some force to subdue. In the energy of overcoming, we are focusing on that which we must overcome, and we thereby create more of it (got it?). We feed the very energy we are wanting to no longer experience. The vibrational opposite of this saying is, "United we stand."

That feels a lot better. Can you see the difference? We can accomplish whatever it is we wish to accomplish by uniting. We are saying energetically, "We are united as one, and as one there can be no vibration other than the one I have come to offer." Accordingly, The Big E delivers – right on schedule as always.

Look at this through your individual perspective. If you must overcome, and you are the creator of your own reality, then you are both the conqueror and the conquered. You are separating from your creative power by placing the blame for your situation on someone else. According to the law of attraction, there is no blame – only the acceptance of responsibility.

In accepting this responsibility and uniting your own vibrations (the vibrations separated in the belief of having to overcome or that there is an outside force at play which you must conquer), you are able to energetically stand and claim your creatorship. Doing so is the first step in achieving anything you wish to achieve.

"Never put off till tomorrow what you could do today."

The only moment we create in is now. When all of our ducks are in a row (and hopefully out of our pool), and resistance creeps in and gets the best of us, we sometimes say to The Big E, "You know what my friend, maybe tomorrow." In that moment, we have said "no" to The Big E; we have said "no" to ourselves. We have vibrationally sent out the command to cease and desist, and The Big E responds accordingly.

We have also unknowingly limited our creation and happiness. We often say to ourselves, "I would be so happy *if* I had that new car. Life would be so much better *if* I could just lose this weight. My life would be perfect *if*..."

Well, *if* is like that guy no one invited to the party. You've got to tell him to leave and be in the vibrations of what you want *now*. If you want that new car, move into the feelings of sliding behind the wheel. Smell that new car smell. Picture yourself driving around town in your new car NOW. Tell The Big E, "I am here, and I am happy now!" so that it can match your vibration with your creation. Love yourself as if you've already lost the weight. Picture your life filled with love.

What this phrase is really saying is, "Say yes to yourself today; Say *yes* to yourself *now*." Find the love inside of yourself now, and allow yourself to open up to life. Don't shut yourself down just as The Big E is ready to bring you your heart's desire. You deserve your good now.

"You Can't Have Your Cake and Eat it Too."

"You can't have your cake and eat it too" goes right to the core of who we are and the limitations we take on and impose upon ourselves. The idea that we can't have what we want and simultaneously enjoy it comes from the belief that we don't deserve all of our good. Through the ages we've been taught not to flaunt what we have – not to enjoy it. We've been taught to keep ourselves small. Basically, we can either have what we want (as long as we don't enjoy it), or we can be happy and remain in want. What good does that do?

Energetically, we are saying to ourselves "I want this/I don't want this" and we are sending out mixed vibrations. This confusion often arises from guilt, judgment, and ultimately not believing we are worthy of our creation. It all comes down to, "Can we love ourselves enough to give ourselves everything we want?"

If everyone had their cake but couldn't eat it, we'd all starve at our own buffets.

Allow yourself to know that you can have everything your heart desires, and that you can enjoy it!

"A Watched Kettle Never Boils."

We're all learning that we bring into our reality whatever we focus on. So, how then do we explain this one? It boils down to (pardon the pun) our attachment to the outcome. If we're peering over the pot from the perspective of "Hurry up and boil already!" it could seem like forever before the water actually boils. So it is with our creation. We know that we create by drawing to us those things that are our vibrational match. So then, if we are trying to create from a place of force – "Hurry up and boil" – our creation may be slow in coming.

Our job is to simply tell The Big E what we want and go on about our business being in joy and gratitude. How The Big E decides to bring it is none of our business. (Think of creation as ordering fast food. Do you order a Big Mac and then freak out wondering if you're actually going to get it?) We don't even need to be in on the planning – E knows what it's doing. I have a friend who always says, "I don't know why they say pregnant women are expecting. They're not expecting anything. They Know!" Energetically, when we "watch the kettle" we are expecting, and our creation is delivered when we move out of the place of expecting, and into the place of knowing.

"Beauty is In the Eye of the Beholder."

The more we learn about energy, the more we realize everything is perspective. To a hungry child, a bowl of coco-puffs is a feast. To a full child, it's extra desert.

You see, we are all the beholders of creation. Everything we see, do, hear, and are, is colored by our perspective. "One man's trash is another man's treasure," because where one man saw trash, the other saw potential. On an energetic level, we are all the same. We are all atoms and molecules, and particles. What we are beyond that is only as good or bad as our own judgment. If I judge myself to be fat, then I am fat, and I will continue to be fat. How do I feel about being fat then? If I love myself as I am, the term "fat" loses its charge, and I love myself as is. If I create someone else coming into my awareness who does not like people he or she deems fat and I am called "fat" as a put-down, will I allow their perspective to shift mine, or will I continue to be the beholder of my own image?

We all have the power to claim ourselves as our beholder, and once this is done, beauty is our choice, and ours alone.

"Up The Creek Without a Paddle"

My fifth grade math teacher used to say this all the time. To him, being up the creek without a paddle pretty much meant, "You're screwed." To my little ten-year-old mind it never made sense. The only creek I had to reference was the small creek behind my neighbor's house. "It's just a creek." I thought. "You don't need a paddle. You really don't even need a boat. Get out and walk." The truth is, even in life's largest creek, you don't need a paddle. You just need to let go.

When we're up the creek without a paddle, most of us think we're stuck or at the mercy of the raging currents of life. It's a metaphor for being stranded with no way of directing our path. The truth is, within the currents of life, our energy is the only paddle we need. If I choose to feel stuck and alone, I will be stuck and alone. But, if I chose to acknowledge the flow, and either give over to it – letting the current take me where it may – or know that I am home no matter where I am – even in that little boat, I will be just fine. The feeling of being stuck is just resistance to the flow. Instead of trying to get back up stream to where you've always been, let go and enjoy the ride. Choose the vibration of love, and your boat will flow exactly where it's supposed to every time. Just be willing to let go of where you *think* your destination is. In giving over, you just may find that the quickest way in life to get to where you truly want to go, is by throwing away the paddle... and remember, it's only a creek.

"Talk of the Devil, and the Devil Appears."

I think I'd rather just shut my mouth then. How about you?

We all know that "What we focus on appears;" it's the Law of attraction in a nutshell, and based on this, we know that the quickest way to create anything is to focus on it. When I first sat down to describe the energy of this statement, I looked at Dee and said, "I'm stuck on the most obvious statement we've got." After I told her the statement, she turned around and said, "So, stop focusing on the devil." Just like that I was unstuck. I was literally focusing on being stuck. It's so simple when you learn to speak the language.

When we focus our attention on something, it's like placing an order with the Big E. By focusing on being stuck, I was ordering a huge plate of stuck (and I'm much more of a pizza guy). By shifting my focus over to writing, I began to write.

This brings up another point. I did not become un-stuck by focusing on *becoming* un-stuck. Rather, I focused on what I wanted, which was to have an explanation of the energy at work behind this statement. Had I focused on not being stuck, I would have continued to create and manifest the energy of being stuck.

It's like this: try not to think of a pink elephant. See?

A great way to illustrate this principle is with the plant from "Little Shop of Horrors." The plant kept yelling to be fed (the plant here being the devil, fear, or anything else you may be focusing on). If they had said "no," the darn thing would have never grown into the monster it became.

"You Can't Have It Both Ways."

We can't?

Well, not vibrationally. That's not to say that we can't have our cake and eat it too - because we can.

What we're really saying is, we can't have our cake, let alone eat it – no matter how badly we consciously want it – while we're energetically holding "I don't deserve it."

We're all pretty complex people, right?

Eh! Wrong. We can let go of that one right now because what most of us are holding as "complex" is our inner struggle between "yes" and "no," and it's the struggle between the two that creates the resistance to creating exactly what we want.

We can't have a house and be homeless at the same time, and vibrationally, most of us are trying to create just that. We're trying to create what we want, while holding the frequencies of both "I want it" and "I don't want it." Once we know we are worth receiving what we want, the polarities of "yes" and "no" (I deserve it/I don't deserve it, I want it/I don't want it) come together in a balanced way. The two vibrations become one direct point of creation, and we are able to not only have our cake, but to enjoying every last bite – which for me is good, because I like cake.

"Knowledge is Power."

To fully understand why "knowledge" is power, we have to have an understanding of true power. Power is not force. Power is not the ability to overcome; it is the ability to just be. It is the ability to know that you are the all and that all is well. The purest form of power lies within each one of us – it is our ability to love ourselves. When we can truly love ourselves, we are able to truly love others. When we know that there is nothing we must change about ourselves in order to be loved, we know that there is nothing we must change about anyone else in order to love them.

Knowledge, then, is not something gained from books or life experience. Rather, it is the extent to which we can allow, trust, and love who we are. We are able to stop taking action for the sake of action, because that is force, not power. Vibrationally, our knowing is sent out to The Big E and is answered in kind. When we truly know and embrace who we are, we are able to sit back and allow the Big E to bring us our good, and we are able to receive it in whatever form it wishes to take. Our knowing also spawns an awakening within the people we encounter. Our love for ourselves gives them permission to love and know themselves, and when we possess that knowledge, we possess the ultimate power.

"Misery Loves Company"

You know why? Miserable company gives us a forum in which we can wallow in our misery. We get to be a victim, and we get to feel either validated or rejected – both of which creates more misery. If our company is miserable, even better! If everyone is miserable, we can all sit around and blame everyone else. I mean, if we're all homeless and poor, there must be *something* wrong with the system, right? It's not our fault, right?

Wrong. By commiserating, we prevent ourselves from looking at our own stuff. In this respect, birds of a feather have not only flocked together because they enjoy their misery, but they've flocked together because they have created being miserable as a way to keep themselves from owning their own stuff. Their misery is their own creation, and it is keeping them from creating anything else.

I can remember getting in trouble in the third grade for not paying attention in choir. Instead of apologizing, I kindly informed the teacher that I was laughing because my friends were making faces behind her – thereby dragging my friends into detention with me. My thinking was twofold:

1) Detention won't be so bad if I have people to share it with, and

2) How can my parents be mad when we ALL got in trouble? Obviously we're not all bad kids... Maybe they'll blame the teacher.

The truth of the matter is, energetically, misery loves any company. If you're miserable, and I walk in doing a little happy dance, you're going to tell me to go shove it. How dare I be so happy?

The gall... but hey, at least I have something else to be miserable about, right?

"Jack of All Trades, Master of None"

This phrase is used in reference to someone who seems to do a lot of things, but who doesn't seem to do any of those things really well. Ultimately, the energy at play here is choice. Can I choose to focus on the trade I am currently plying? Can I love myself enough to know that I can be master of all I choose to experience?

You see, most of us define success in life, by how good we are at our job, how much money we make, what kind of relationships we have, even by the amount of happiness we experience on a day-to-day basis, but "Jack of all trades, master of none," implies that by diversifying our interests, we somehow water down our overall mastery of life. It implies that we can't have it all without sacrificing mastery. The truth is, the more we experience, the more we master – because we are the creators of our universe. We create our own E.

Take He-man for example. You know what I liked about He-Man? He was *master* of the entire *freakin'* universe. It even said so below his name. How cool is that? He went through life whipping out his sword at the first sign of trouble, and boldly proclaiming to The Universe, "I have the power!" It didn't matter what the situation was, as long as he had his sword, he had the ability to summon forth all the mastery he needed to complete whatever goal he set before himself.

You and I have that power too. We all have an energetic sword called desire. Desire is the pool from which all creation pours, and by choosing to allow our desire to be limitless, we allow ourselves to experience – to master – all that we choose to call into our creation. All we have to do is claim it, direct it, and allow.

"No Man is an Island."

This phrase is used to illustrate the idea that no man can stand alone. When we look at it literally however, we realize that a better way to say it is that "all men are islands."

Huh?

Don't worry. You didn't miss a memo about opposite day.

Let us show you what we're talking about:

Islands are landmasses surrounded on all sides by water (thank you Miriam Webster for that titillating bit of phraseology), but at their core – at the very depths from which they spring – they are just giant mountains popping up from the bottom of the sea. You see, no matter how deep the water is, when you get to the bottom, there's just more land. The whole earth is just covered in the stuff.

We are all inter-acting with each other whether we know it or not. In fact, like the islands, we are all inter-connected. We are not separate entities floating through life – peering out above the water's surface. We are large bodies of mass living within and among other bodies of mass. Physically, we are people, living on a planet that exists in a solar system, which is part of a galaxy, and so on. On a scientific level, we are the composition of millions of molecules, electrons, and atoms living on an even bigger collection of molecules, atoms and electrons. On the level of quantum physics, we are all vibration. We are vibrations living within a vibration, living within a vibration, and so on. No man is an island because on a scientific and vibrational level, we're all one.

"Nothing Ventured, Nothing Gained"

"Nothing ventured, nothing gained" is not the same vibration as "no pain, no gain." It is simply the belief that in order to gain something, we must venture out. Now, I used to look at this phrase and think it meant, "You've got to take a risk." As a matter of fact, I'm pretty sure it's one of the things I told myself just before losing a substantial amount of money playing "war" in Las Vegas.

What I failed to realize however, was the simplicity in the statement. Think of it this way: If you don't ask, you don't receive, and we have to remember that we are always asking. We are constantly shooting out little vibrational IM's to The Big E, which the Big E always answers – 'cause that's his style.

We are in a constant state of receiving, and what we are receiving is exactly what we are vibrationally asking for. When we can become conscious of what our vibrations are "venturing out" for, we can move from subconscious creation or even our old default ways of being and receiving and move into consciously creating what we want. The best way to know your pattern of venture is to look at your pattern of reception. If you are not where you would like to be, dare to consciously venture out in this moment, and claim what you want.

"One Doctor Makes Work For Two."

We see doctors for a myriad of reasons, but the most basic reason is, we just don't know. If we're sick, we don't know how to be well. If we're well, we don't know how much longer we can keep it up. We live in a society where we're constantly being bombarded with messages of sickness:

"Do you have a big toe? Do you sometimes stub it? You need Toe-No!" Warning: Toe-No may cause the development of severe gas in public places, acid reflux, the inability to pronounce the number seven, and mild heartburn. In some cases, Toe-No did absolutely nothing except cause more worry and panic. If you experience more worry and panic, please see your doctor as it could be the sign of something much more serious and deadly."

After hearing about Toe-No, I may feel a little anxiety creep in. Do I need Toe-No? You know, probably not, but that anxiety thing... my heart seems like it's been beating a little fast lately. Enter the cardiologist who tells me that everything seems fine, but that I seemed to be breathing a little heavy after running on the treadmill for four hours.

"It's probably nothing," he says, "but maybe you should go see Bill down in Pulmonology."

Oh crap. He's right. What if my lungs are bad?

It's usually about this time that my mind starts racing to come up with as many possible reasons as to why my lungs could be bad: Maybe I have asthma. Could it be a food allergy? I knew I shouldn't have eaten that candy bar four months ago. Oh my gosh! I smoked a cigarette in seventh grade. Oh my Word! What if I have cancer? Bill? Where's Bill?

Someone find me Bill so he can tell me I'm fine.

Some of us do it the opposite way too. We spend our entire lives trying to be sick.

Hey, Susie; how are you?

Great... but you know my hip has been acting up.

Susie, the doctor said your hip was fine.

Oh, what does he know?

I'm reminded of the famous quote by Henry Ford, "Whether you think you can or you think you can't, you're right."

The only doctor who can ultimately heal you is you. Sure, you may put your faith in the medicine he gives you, and you may put your faith in him, but ultimately the choice to heal is yours.

How many times have you heard a TV doctor say, "We did all that we could. The rest is up to him?"

In China, there are people who have surgery under no anesthetic. Instead, they have acupuncture. Personally, if you're gonna open me up, I want you to knock me out. You know why? Because I don't believe that acupuncture could put me under – and as I believe, so shall I receive.

"One doctor makes work for two" whether that other doctor is actually another doctor or whether it is you. Ultimately, the creation for all things lies within. "Physician heal thyself" is not just directed at doctors, it is directed to us all.

"Out of Sight, Out of Mind."

Well, this is pretty much the inverse law of attraction. If you're not focused on something, it's not gonna be in your face. The statement is really saying the obvious. If we take something out of our surroundings – whether it's a funky relationship, a bottle of alcohol, an abusive husband, whatever – we're much less likely to dwell on it or obsess about it. It's one of the reasons dieticians tell people going on a diet to get all the junk food out of the house. If you open your pantry and all you see is peanut butter cupcakes, while at the same time, you're trying *not* to eat peanut butter cupcakes, all you're gonna be thinking about is eating or not eating that peanut butter cupcake. Either way, you're focus is on the cupcake.

Energetically, "out of site" is the result of "out of mind." Things come in to our environment as a reflection of our thoughts. Alcoholics have a saying that "first the man takes the drink, and then the drink takes the man." The drink takes the man because the man is constantly focused on the drink. Bowling, exercise, and all the hobbies in the world won't change that fact unless the decision is made to do those things because you truly want to have the experience of those things. Doing things out of avoidance is vibrationally closer to your goal, but it is still holding the polarity of your desire. You are doing something in order not to do something else. Your focus is split.

What we have to remember to do is to stay focused on the positive and stay focused on what we want. If you don't want to drink, what do you want?

You want to lead a happy, sober life. If you don't want to eat peanut butter cupcakes, what do you want? You want to eat healthy and enjoy it.

"Paddle Your Own Boat"

You are the only one who can create for you. You are the only one responsible for you. Most of us can get to these points with fairly little resistance. We sometimes have a harder time marrying our creation with the creation of others. We want to "fix" other people, and the honest truth is they aren't broken.

We think, well, I can see where your life is going wrong, now just do what I tell you and you'll be fine.

The truth is, you are not responsible for them – never were.

Sure, as a parent, you are the person who feeds your child, but beyond that, their choices are their choices. You can guide them, but eventually they will grow up, and you won't be able to control them.

Know that it's all good, and allow everyone the freedom of their choices. Besides, just as the only person who can change you is you, the only person who can change them, is them.

Think of life like a small canoe. You can go wherever you want to, but when you sidle up next to someone else and try to paddle their boat, not only can you not do it, but *your* boat has now become wobbly. Your attempt to paddle their boat has caused yours to rock.

You cannot create your mother-in-law being nicer to you. All you can do is be who you are, and release the rest. Ever heard the one about the bird that was let go but winds up coming back? It's like that. Let go of the idea that you have to change people. Allow them the freedom to choose what they want. It's like Gandhi said, "Be the change you wish to see in the world." Be that change for you.

When you can let go of paddling everyone else's boat, I think you'll find the river is a much easier place to flow.

"People Who Live In Glass Houses Shouldn't Throw Stones."

...Especially with the price of windows these days.

We're all a part of the same energy. We are all here experiencing what it is like to be an individualized expression of Source Energy.

We all have desires, and those desires fuel our creation, but we have to remember, our desires are just that – they are *ours*. They do not belong to everybody. The same principal applies to our values, our religious beliefs, and our entire upbringing. We have the desires we have, because they have come from our individualized experiences. Everyone has different experiences. Everyone perceives the world through his or her own eyes.

Give yourself the freedom to release judgment – judgment of others, and most importantly, judgment of yourself. When we can all accomplish this, the only things people will be throwing are parties.

People who live in glass houses shouldn't throw stones because it isn't necessary. Live your life – create your life, and allow others the freedom to do the same. "Live and let live" as they say, and feel free to walk around barefoot. There's no broken glass in a house of love.

"Power Corrupts While Absolute Power Corrupts Absolutely."

I've never particularly heard this phrase used outside of politics, but the overall vibration here is negative, negative, negative.

If I believe that power corrupts, not only will I attract corruptible people into my life who are in positions of power (boo), but I myself will refuse to empower myself – because when I have power, I will be corrupted. If I own the total creatorship of my world, I will be absolutely corrupted and something bad will happen (that's no good). Therefore, the pattern that emerges is one wherein I perceive myself to be powerless in the face of corrupt leaders. When I own my power, I too become corrupt... I can't win.

We need to let this one go, stat!

We not only have the power to focus upon and create whatever we wish to experience (yes!), but we also have the power to judge it. Through judgment, mistrust, and the act of giving away our power, we may have come to the conclusion that power corrupts. What we have to know is that the only way to achieve whatever it is we wish to achieve is by fully embracing our power and by fully embracing our selves – for who we are is truly powerful (double yes!). We have to embrace absolutely that our thoughts, attitudes, etc – ergo: our energy – shapes and creates our outer world and experiences – and as Martha says, "that's a good thing."

"Tomorrow is Another Day."

When I was younger, I loved playing video games (and by younger, I mean I still play them). When it came to fighting games, almost every kid I knew had the same move. I'm not talking about a punch combo; I'm talking about "accidentally" hitting reset anytime their character was close to eating it. Now that I'm grown up (mostly), I kind of view this as the ultimate creation move. If you don't like the way something is going, press reset on your energy.

You see, all we have is this moment, and this moment is the moment from which all others will come. Now is the only moment in which we can create. "Tomorrow" is actually a metaphor for the moment of now because tomorrow truly is another day, and I can choose to create whatever I want tomorrow. Tomorrow will be a new "now," and I am always free to leave behind my baggage and start anew in the moment.

We are always in the moment of creation, and if at any time we find that what we are creating is no longer what we want, we can hit reset and start fresh.

It's not like we don't know how to create. We're creating right now. The point of this proverb is to let us know that we don't ever have to get too bogged down in anything. We can choose to create from a blank slate in any moment. The choice is ours as to whether or not we will drag our past along with us, or we will truly let it be a new, fresh day.

If we can live the belief that tomorrow is another day, we will always be free. We will be able to leave our stories behind. We are free to create in the moment, and we release the vibrations that have been creating the things we do not want. When we know that we are always free to create something else, we are freed from feelings of helplessness, victimness, and bondage.

When we just surrender and allow, we are free to change what we're creating, and we are free to move on to whatever desire comes next.

"Too Many Cooks Spoil the Broth."

If we're all eating out of the same pot, we have to agree on what to put in the broth, right? Well, not really. This may be true within the context of cooking, but it is not true in creation.

"Yes, but we don't live in a bubble."

Well, that's true too (kind of). We all interact and mingle with each other's energy, but *our* creation *is our* bubble. Who we mix with is our choice. If I invite seven chefs over to cook one pot of soup, am I going to invite someone who is allergic to salt, a salt-a-holic, someone with no taste, someone who hates spicy food, someone who refuses to eat anything other than spicy food, someone who has the tendency to make stew instead of soup, and someone who doesn't even like soup?

Of course not.

My life is my pot. I can allow other people to put stuff in, but ultimately, I'm the only one who is in charge of what goes in. I may allow something in out of fear or sacrifice, but it's still my call. If I don't like the broth, I'm the only one responsible.

I have to remember that I am the only one who can create for me. Other people have ideas, but those ideas are for their soup, not mine (I'm talking to you, Brussels sprouts!). I have to remember what *I* like, and know that I have a responsibility to my self to make it that way.

Bottom line: Don't spoil your broth by giving away your pot.

"No Man Can Serve Two Masters"

This phrase falls into the same category as "a house divided," meaning you can't serve yourself and serve the limitations of everybody else at the same time. Neither can you truly serve yourself while trying to serve *your own* limitations. Lost? (Me too.)

Let's look at it this way:

The Big E simply gets, places, and tries to deliver your order. If we're telling The Big E that we want a successful relationship, yet we're holding the belief that we have to put our work before our relationships – and we have a job we love – we are trying to serve two masters. "E" goes, "Well, they love their job, so keep that coming... but oh, they want a relationship too. What do I do?" In this example, we are trying to serve the part of ourselves that wants a relationship, while at the same time trying to honor and serve the limited part of us that thinks a relationship is going to be in conflict with a job.

Kids have a hard time with this one too, because so often they sacrifice themselves to make their parents happy. We see it in Little League all the time. The kids are there to have fun, but mom or dad wants them to win. They then become conflicted. "Well, I had fun, but they wanted me to win, so I guess I have to give up the fun part and start taking this more seriously." Growing up with this belief, it wouldn't be too far of a stretch to become a successful professional who hates their job.

When we can allow ourselves the freedom to be who we are, we move into servitude of the only person on this planet that has the ability to choose our happiness – us.

"Just Whistle A Happy Tune."

When we're in the dumps, friends can pick us up.

When we're feeling down, a great comedy can help us turn our sadness around.

Personally, when my husband died, I went to get my toes done.

You know why?

It made me feel better!

Feeling good just feels... better! After all, we all like to laugh, love, and create, right?

Hmmm...

We know that in order to lead a happy life, we want to focus on a happy tune, but often we choose the drama anyway.

Why?

Well, we get confused. The drama feels like a roller coaster ride of excitement, but the truth is that as long as we need that excitement in our lives, we're never going to get off the ride. We'll continue to need our fix, which will just create more drama.

By whistling a happy tune, we can choose to tap dance, chill out, or vibe anywhere we'd like because *happy* is the vibration that attracts *more happy*.

So jump off the drama ride, and come hang out with happy ☺.

"Always Look On The Brighter Side Of Life."

I don't know about you, but I certainly wouldn't go to McDonald's and expect a total stranger to just bring me whatever they thought I'd like. Nope. I prefer to check out the menu and place my order based on my own individual preferences.

It's a silly example, but the point is: You must choose. We know it when we're ordering a hamburger, so why don't we know it with everything else?

Instead of telling the Big E what we want, most of us are sitting back and not choosing. And guess what? If we don't choose, somebody else chooses for us... Hope you like liver and onions.

If we are not *choosing* to see life through our own joyous perspectives, we are allowing everyone else – the victims, the hateful, the angry and the judgmental – to order for us. If we are not consciously *choosing* happiness, love, and laughter, the rest of the world gets to order for us, and we have to keep eating whatever vibrations are thrown our way. By choosing the thoughts and experiences we want to feel, we're energetically coming forward and ordering from our own menu, and I don't know about you, but I'm starting with dessert.

"I Used To Think I Had It Bad Because I Had No Shoes...Then I Met A Man Who Had No Feet."

This is really a "no-brainer;" it's simply about gratitude.

Do we necessarily want to have the experience of having no feet?

That would be a "no."

The question is: "Could we still live in gratitude if that were our experience?"

"Could we be grateful for the discount shoes we're wearing as well as the Gucci sandals we'd love to have?" If we can't, those Guccis will keep getting further and further away from manifesting in our lives.

True "gratitude" is having an awesome appreciation of the wonder of creation, and when we can *truly* live in gratitude, our heart centers open, and we live in love. This is important because love cancels out fear, judgment, and guilt. Self-love allows us to see and celebrate everything from the perspective of Divine Love, which fills us up and sends out more vibrations of love.

The Beach Boys knew what they were singing about when they sang "Good Vibrations." When we say, "Thank you" to Big E, The Big E gives us even more to be thankful for.

So, everybody on 3:

1-2-3: Thank You!!!

"You Can Lead A Horse To Water, But You Can't Make Him Drink."

You simply cannot create for another person. You can lead them to classes, or buy them books, or even give them guided meditations and chant for them, but their creation, ultimately, lies within their own directions and choice. If someone is holding the belief that "no matter what I do, it doesn't work," no amount of pushing or passive suggestion will make a difference. They have to want to change – or at the very least, be willing to think change is a possibility.

As a parent, this knowledge can be frightening. Yes, we can guide, and teach, and push our children to do what we feel is right, but ultimately, whatever they choose is their choice. Whether they become the horse that drinks or the horse that – even though it was led to water – dies from thirst, is their decision and their creation.

The same principal applies to alcoholics and addicts.

We can love, encourage, and support until we're worn out, but the ultimate choice to change must always come from them.

They have to choose.

Love yourself enough to honor yourself and everyone else. Don't mistake another's lessons for your own. Be kind to your fellow man, but know that even though you can lead them to water, it is their choice to drink or go thirsty.

"When Life Gives You Lemons, Make Lemonade."

The power of this statement lies in its vibrational truth. We all know that our energy is made up of frequencies that vibrate out into the world. Those vibrations magnetically attract other like-vibrations. In other words, negative vibrations will attract negativity, while positive vibrations will attract positive experiences. Hate pushes away and excludes, while love invites and embraces.

If life gives us something we perceive as negative, and we go into re-action, we move out of creation. We begin fighting the flow with our judgment, our ego, and the "lower" vibrations of hate, disappointment and fear. When we are able to take that same occurrence and remain in love and trust, we can literally create something better. In changing our perception, we can move from re-action, to action – which is how we create the very things we want.

When life gives us lemons (or what we perceive to be negative things), we have to make the decision to stay balanced and create something positive.

Remember, lemonade stands *always* make money.

"If At First You Don't Succeed...
Try, Try Again."

There are both positive and negative messages here.

If at first you don't succeed, try, try again – IF

Your vibrations and energy are positive and joyful.

Your learning curve has caught up with your dream.

You're not daring yourself to NOT succeed.

Trying again is good – unless there is unhappy, despondent, "what's the use" energy. If the "try again" is laborious, we might as well not waste our time. If we didn't learn what we needed to learn to enhance our success the second (or third!) time, we're no smarter than the mouse that sticks to the same route in the maze over and over and never gets the cheese. The poor little guy has tenacity – but he never gets what he wants.

Love yourself enough to give yourself what you want, and don't go after it if it's not YOUR dream. Remember, you create your life, so create what *you* want.

"If It Ain't Broke...Don't Fix It."

Basically, don't bring negative, lower vibrations into a place with balanced vibrations.

We create what we focus on. Focus on something (or someone!) that we perceive needs fixing, and that's what we will keep creating: more to be fixed.

If someone is happy *just the way they are,* leave them alone. Their "happy" may not be your "happy," but it doesn't have to be. Be happy that they're happy.

If a situation is balanced and maintained in a healthy way (i.e. it ain't broke), bless it, and enjoy it.

We drive ourselves daily to "fix" things by making more money, or losing weight, or trying to look younger, but with the added focus of joy and happiness, how many of those things truly matter?

Our job is to be happy, period. Instead of "what can I fix," look at "what am I happy with right now?" What's whole, right, and good with my world?

In other words, look at what ain't broke, and celebrate!

"Progress, Not Perfection"

It's so important for us to realize that we are a process. We are all miracles in the making. In every single moment of every single day, we are becoming – and what we are becoming is up to us. Sometimes though, we get discouraged or bogged down in our thinking.

"Why am I not there yet?"

The truth is, there is no "there." Everything is right here in the present moment, and when you can stay joyful and mindful and experience the present, you'll simply begin to experience a sense of newness and continuation of the present.

"Yes, but I'm in the present, and I'm in my joy; so why isn't this happening for me?"

Think of it this way: If your goal is to count to ten, and you begin counting, are you going to stop at the number five and ask, "Why am I not to ten yet?" or are you going to continue counting, knowing that you are heading in the exact direction of accomplishment?

So many times we get caught up looking for the perfection and the manifestation of our desires (or judging ourselves or others in their absence) that we actually alter the process without consciously knowing it. Our focus shifts from "This is so much fun," and "It would be so cool if..." to "Why isn't this working?" and "Where's my stuff?" When we shift our focus, we shift our outcome.

Don't get caught up in the details. Instead, enjoy the process. Ask, and let go – knowing that you have already done your job.

"Be Careful What You Wish For, You Might Just Get It"

This one is a doozie (and also the chorus to a pretty good Pussycat Dolls song).

Clearly, we can't create something *consciously* if we don't know what we want to create. So be clear, and then allow the Big E to play with you in the creation of whatever it is. However, if you are *not* clear and *not consciously* choosing what you want, everything else around you will do your creating in haphazard ways.

Your subconscious picks up conflicting messages from the media, limiting messages from parents, fearful messages from partners etc. that become your vibrations which create your life and YOU DON'T EVEN KNOW IT.

Even in this saying is the subconscious message that you might hate what you really want – that getting what you *really* want might make you really unhappy. I ask you, HAS THAT BEEN YOUR EXPERIENCE?

There is a simple default: want everything you want with Love.

If you don't create your life, you become the created upon.

"Penny Saved Is A Penny Earned."

Double-edged message again – and probably one that Donald Trump disagrees with. He SPENDS money to earn money. Wealthy people come from a wealth consciousness, not the fear that if you spend you'll lose.

If you go to Vegas and take "a safe amount to lose," the vibration/expectation/message is "I'll be okay to lose this much."

On the other hand (warning: perspective change), honoring yourself by *giving* to yourself in the form of saving, is a great vibration as long as it isn't based in fear and lack. To save "in case of a rainy day" can be both positive and negative.

To save, knowing you are always safe and taken care of with the expectation of doing great things for yourself, is an entirely different vibration than being scared to death you'll die homeless and have nothing. You stash everything away – which keeps you *living* in lack and fear, which creates that in your life.

Always be aware of the intention around why you do things. Is it joyful, loving, nurturing and heart centered?

The lucky penny in your life can create more than $100 in the bank if it makes you smile every time you look down.

"All's Well That Ends Well."

A pretty limited description of happiness, don't you think?

If our definition of things being positive depends on their final outcome, none of us are enjoying the ride. And the ride IS the creation. It is in every moment of the ride that the end creation is created!

We have all been taught to focus on the win, the achievement, the final victory – the manifestation – and sometimes, this takes us out of the appreciation of actually creating. It takes us out of the moments of gratitude, love, excitement, and imagination that are the very vibrations needed for all to "end well."

The ultimate sweet spot for manifestation is that place where we can focus on WHAT WE WANT while we are participating in every moment of its creation. We need to live and breathe (and vibrate) as if we already have it – while we joyfully experience every moment of the journey.

Look at it like this: If you want a piece of candy you think you can't get, the time between now and when you eventually do or do not get it isn't going to be much fun. Know that you can get the candy, and then enjoy every sneaky, fun step along the way.

"This Too Shall Pass."

Everything does. It's a law. Energy is forever expanding and changing. Nothing stays the same – even the stuff that appears to be exactly the same. We can live ninety different, unique years, or we can live the same year over and over for ninety years – either way, every day is going to be different, whether we acknowledge it or not.

So when there is a physical, mental or emotional "problem" (we prefer "challenge") that comes into our lives, what we want to do is focus on the happy solution – and happiness is always a choice.

Illness comes so we can learn about healing ourselves. Where do we need to nurture and love ourselves more?

Money problems? Focus on HAVING MONEY, while being in gratitude for the money you already have.

So yes, know "it" will pass. Allow "it" to pass not by focusing on "it" going away, but by focusing on what you want. Love yourself enough to CHOOSE to honor and support yourself with high and happy vibrations.

When you can do this, the "it" that could have stayed for a year might just pass in a week.

"Pride Comes Before The Fall."

Obviously, this was written by someone who wanted to take another person's power away.

So what? Don't love myself? Don't be proud of my accomplishments, and don't be filled up or bursting with pride?

What about my kids?

Hmmm. I guess I shouldn't be too proud of them either.

The message in this little ditty is, "if you love what you do and acknowledge how great you are, you are going to lose – BIG TIME!"

Well, mister cliché writer, sorry – not in my experience!

Feeling great about yourself is the perfect way to create more great things. It opens your heart and expands your joy.

The choice here is whether or not you want to live in joy and expansion, or seriousness and victim-hood.

Creation is fun. It's love. It's – YIPEE! Anything (i.e. the above statement) that takes that away from you and makes you feel "wrong" is a place you don't want to go. Walk the other way, or choose a different person to chat with.

Remember, the most important person in this equation is *You*, so don't worry; just be happy.

Beggars Can't Be Choosers

Here's why: If we are begging, we are in victim energy, and we definitely aren't coming forward to claim what we want. Most of the time, when we're in this energy, we can't even imagine *getting* what we want because we have given our creation away to everyone else and whatever "grace" may come our way. In this instance, we have lost our self-love and our self-respect – two big ingredients in balance and choice.

When we lose sight of the fact that only we create our lives, it is easy to blame the world for not showing up for us. Blame gives us an out. We stop choosing. We give up. When we regain our knowing, we're able to go, "Oh yeah, the buck stops here."

There is no one else responsible for anything in your life, other than you. There is also no situation you need to be saved from – unless that's the situation that you've created.

Sometimes, it's easier not to have any choices because then we don't have to make decisions, and we don't have to be responsible for anything one way or the other.

In doing this, we also lose the right, the power, and the *choice* to create. We can't beg someone to love us. We must love ourselves first, so that someone else can then show up and mirror back that love. Our boss can't respect our work or us, until we begin respecting ourselves.

Like-wise, the Big E can't match-up victim energy with a victorious life.

No more begging. It's time to take life back. Reclaim your responsibility, and reclaim your right to happiness. The first steps – just like all the rest – are up to you.

"You Can't Teach An Old Dog New Tricks."

Well, you can *if* the dog chooses to learn some new ones!

But most of us dogs like to hold on to the chew toys we know. Don't throw me a ball, don't make me chase a Frisbee. Give me the same old stuff with the same old limitations that BORE me but keep me safe. I have control over my life with those chew toys!

If we are going to expand into all those new dreams – money, fame, health, relationships, etc. – we have to choose to play with different vibrations and beliefs (possibly even more exciting/scary ones). We have to choose to create some new tricks for ourselves because we love ourselves so much that we want to expand out of our comfortable backyards.

And the first person that has to teach you – IS you. Even if your first step is teaching yourself to buy a self help book, take a class, find a mentor, listen to your beliefs and fears, journal – whatever!

Throw that Frisbee out there and go chase it. Chase it with tail flying and tongue wagging and legs leaping with joy. You might even jump so high you get over the fence.

"What You Think Is What You Get."

Wow! They actually had it right with this one. I'll take this over "money doesn't grow on trees" any day!

This is the basis for all of the "New" messages, "The Secret," and even "What the Bleep": What we think about – *consciously* or *unconsciously* – will be brought into our lives.

As Henry Ford said, "Whether you think you can or you think you can't, you're right." In other words, what you think about, you create!

If you're watching TV and being bombarded with hundreds of messages of sickness, fear, and crime, and you are *not consciously redirecting* those images and messages, you are creating them as a reality in your life. Why? Because you are passively accepting them.

Think only about what you want. Don't think about what you don't want. Be joyous in directing the Universe to walk with you into manifesting it all.

Share your time with other conscious creators. Heck, take a few minutes and make an image board – whatever makes you feel GOOD. After all, you get what you think about, so:

Think Big. Think Positive. Think Love!

"Every Cloud Has a Silver Lining."

This is a true statement IF you are conscious enough to find it (the silver lining that is). Unfortunately, many of us stay so focused on the clouds and wait in expectation of the impending storm that we prolong the agony, never allow the sun to break, and therefore, the silver lining never gets its reflection to shine. What you don't look for doesn't appear. What you focus on, you get.

If we call all of life "good" instead of the "bad" cloud and the "good" silver lining, we see that all life is serving us to get to where we want to be. It is a journey, and just being here and exploring and loving IS the silver lining.

When something we perceive as "negative" happens, if we can accept it with wonder, celebrate what we get to learn about the human experience, choose to focus on what we want ('cause now we're *very* clear about what we *don't* want) and be happy on our journey to create it, all life becomes a silver lining.

Change your perspective and change your life. Look for the silver lining. The clouds pass by much more quickly.

"God Cures, And The Physician Takes The Fee."

I wish we'd heard this more. We'd all be a lot healthier –especially if we understood that "God" is just another name for pure and loving Source Energy. Everything that is, is energy; it's all God (or Love, or Big E, or Creative Force... whatever your term), and we are all *that* one energy – and that One Energy is available and capable to cure everything.

Look at it this way: in some cases, sugar pills have just as much effect as pharmaceuticals. People with multiple personalities often have different problems depending on which personality (energy/belief system) is dominant, i.e. one personality will have diabetes and the other won't. One personality is near sighted; the other has 20-20 vision. So again, sickness extends beyond the physical part of the body. It's in the perception and belief of what we Believe We Can Create and Heal.

So, if a physician/healer/guru/shaman, etc. can help you heal through your belief, they are invaluable to you. Just be conscious that your own Energy directs and chooses the unconditional healing. You give yourself permission to embrace the challenge, love the challenge, and recreate your reality.

Love that body, baby! Love yourself enough to heal.

"He Who Hesitates Is Lost."

Intuition! It's all about intuition, baby. And fear.

We have to have a clear intention to manifest anything. Intention is the first step to taking the first step. It is our self direction to begin action. And it usually comes from intuition: a hit, an idea, or even an awesome "aha."

Intuition is a quiet, quick little sucker. Sometimes it says hello and goodbye within seconds. And it never knocks you in the head like a V-8 moment. It suggests and teases. And oftentimes we don't hear and pay attention. But when we do, we get gold. Intuition is the Universal Gold being delivered into our consciousness. We have to mine it in that moment – or it's gone.

If we dismiss our ideas as being whimsical, dismiss ourselves at not knowing how to implement the idea, dismiss the world as a place that won't want the idea – we hesitate, stall out, and no gold is mined.

Fear is the greatest ally in hesitation. Fear keeps us from trusting ourselves so we never take that first step. We hesitate.

Seize the moment. If you get an idea, dig that mine until you get the gold. Keep asking, "How can I?" Find the creative you that you may have lost by taking action!

"Half A Loaf Is Better Than None."

This is really a perspective challenge. It depends on if you see the glass half full or half empty. If you are a homeless person who is hungry, a half a loaf is an E-send. He is grateful for any amount of sustenance and especially if he doesn't have to pay for it.

On the other hand, the woman throwing a dinner party for fifty isn't going to be too happy if only a half a loaf shows up. No matter how much she has to pay for it.

The vibration behind this can either be one of gratitude for what one has received, or one of lack of consciousness in accepting less than you want. You know, the "I might as well settle for half if I can't get the whole thing" vibration.

Again, we see the importance of perspective. But my guess would be that even the homeless man would rather have a whole loaf. He could always save it for a rainy day.

"Health Is Better Than Wealth."

Okay. WHY DO WE HAVE TO CHOOSE? I mean, really, its apples and oranges here. The premise of this statement suggests you can't have both. I want both. I deserve both. I'm HAPPY when I have both.

It's like you can't have your cake and eat it, too. What's the darn good of having the cake, then?

I think the vibrations of joy and love create both things. I love myself enough to be healthy. I love myself enough to be wealthy. I love myself enough to create all of what I desire to manifest in a balanced good.

Wealth can buy you the greatest medical care to create/recreate your healthy state of being. Health creates a body and mind that gives you the opportunity to create wealth.

Personally, I don't want to give up part of myself so I feel okay to get another part of myself. I want it all. I want all choices. Life is a banquet: a healthy, wealthy, smorgasbord of a banquet.

"Desperate Times Call For Desperate Measures."

This one is kind of like trying to put out a fire by smothering it with gasoline.

This statement is literally inviting us to FOCUS on the desperate times, be VICTIMS OF the desperate times, and LIVE IN THE VIBRATION of the desperate times!

We know that to create the opposite, positive manifestation we DON'T focus on what we don't want: we focus only on what we *do* want – happy times! We don't wallow in the victimness because that gives AWAY our creation of the happy times. And we certainly know we need to live in loving, joyful vibrations to create more of the happy times!

No wonder we are having such a tough time really "getting" it. Most of us have been taught the very opposite of true creation since birth. We have been taught non-creation, or "How to Create What You Don't Want." AKA: Desperate Lives. Desperate Times call for love, joy, and peace held *within* each individual. Then there will be no times of desperation to recreate.

"Birds Of A Feather Flock Together."

Vibrations attract like, or similar, vibrations. You won't find people who are positive and creating abundance and joy having a beer together and talking about how crummy life is. You might, however, find them having a beer and laughing about the money they just made, or the fun they have with each other.

This saying simply refers to the fact that we flock where there is the least resistance to who we are. Take a look at your life. Who hangs out in your space? Are they successful, happy, healthy, creative, and excited about life? If not, then take a moment to reflect within. What are you holding about yourself that is not taking you into the flock of those vibrations? Do you feel comfortable there? Judged? Not as good as...

Where we gather and who we gather with says a lot about what belief and vibrations we hold about ourselves.

Do we love ourselves enough to choose what is empowering and joyful for ourselves – first?

If you want to soar with eagles, you have to know you can. And vultures feel powerful by feeding off dead energy. What group do you choose to flock with?

"Fools Rush In Where Angels Fear To Tread."

Personally, I don't think angels fear to tread anywhere. They have nothing to lose; they've already made it.

I do, however, think they choose vibrations that they resonate with, and therefore, do not rush in to match the fool who still doesn't get it.

The fool still lives in the land where it is everybody else's fault. He is a victim of circumstance, he has no control over his life or destiny, and he lives in fear and reaction to what is happening – or is going to.

If I were an angel, I wouldn't be rushing into those vibes either. I'd be directing my little wings the opposite direction.

Fools look where the energy is going to support them in all their limitations and fearfulness. They are Attracted To It and Attract It To Them as confirmation that they are right. And they get to be. They just don't get what they want.

I want to be a light and airy angel. I want to be peaceful and full of love for myself and everyone else. I want the quiet knowingness that all is working together for the highest good. Attract *THAT* TO ME, AND ME TO IT.

I will not fear to tread in bliss. I will allow the fool his choice, and know it doesn't affect mine.

"Forewarned Is Forearmed."

Whew! Can you feel the expectation of fear here?

Alert! Trouble may be coming!

Alert! Prepare for the worst.

Alert! If you know what's coming, you can be prepared in advance to fight.

This keeps us in the ever-so-popular fight or flight vibration – not conducive to relaxing and letting the flow happen.

What we expect, we focus on, usually from fear of getting/not getting it. And what we focus on, we create more of. In this case, the expectation of something we better be ready for – and it ain't good!

Some might argue that this is simply a declaration of preparedness. Why not, then, Self-Creation is Forearmed. After all, nothing is being done TO us. It's all being created BY us. If we don't know that, I guess we DO want to forewarn ourselves against – ourselves. Hmmm.

Don't think being afraid of yourself is going to help you move into self-love and empowerment. Better to choose your creation and be prepared to get everything you desire. Would it be okay with you if your life got easier?

"If Everybody Jumped Off A Cliff, Would You?"

I think this was my mother's favorite. And this one she had right.

Mom! Everyone else is wearing bikinis!

Dee-Dee, if everybody else...

Mom! Everyone else is getting a tattoo

...If everybody...

But everyone else is sleeping over at the coed party

Well, If everybody else... You get the picture.

Basically, Mom was encouraging me to think for myself and create my own life. I hated it then. I *love* it now.

By creating for myself, I get to disregard the constants messages that:

1)   1 out of 3 women will get breast cancer

2)   I have to take chemical medication to heal *anything*

3)   Terrorists are taking over the world

4)   Global warming is irreversible and we're all going to drown or fry.

I mean, the list goes on an on. Those are the people jumping off the proverbial cliff. Do you want to blindly follow? Or, perhaps, maybe say, "Thanks, mom; you were right?"

I'm not going to follow. I'm going to lead. I will not jump. I will *leap* into knowing that *I* create my world, and when I jump, my wings appear!

"Do What You Love And The Money Will Follow."

There are so many reasons this saying is true; I almost don't know where to begin. Luckily for all of us, I said "*Almost!*"

First of all, doing what you love means you have made a choice to love yourself. You are doing what feeds your soul.

Doing what you love gives you joy, and the very reason we are here is to be joyous!

Next, know that joy creates joyful, happy, fulfilled, loving vibrations that float out into the world and make people feel good because then THEY get to experience your excitement and love. That triggers the same vibrations of love in *them*, and they SEND THOSE BACK TO YOU. Now we have a circle of excited, creative, loving vibrations coming back to us (and then going out again *from* us) on a continual basis.

When you put a dollar exchange on that excited creativity, you make money. But the *original* vibration was love of what you do.

Often, when we go to the making of money *first,* we lose the very vibrations that really create excitement, love and creativity.

Do what you love, share it with the world, and know that that exchange is worth the energy of money you get back! Everybody wins.

"God Helps Him Who Helps Himself."

I hope you have a new understanding of this by the end of the page.

Everything is energy; we learned that in fifth grade.

There is no separation of energy. We can break any solid matter down into the same basic electrons, neutrons, and even atoms. At the teensy, tiniest levels of science, everything looks the same; it is all One Energy.

People call The Big E by many names, all according to their own beliefs and practices, but The Big E is that energy. *We* are that Energy.

So it's all about direction, baby!!

The Big E can't help us if we don't help ourselves by opening up to the energy and vibrations of what we truly want; the change has to start within. We have to love and open up to ourselves and let The Big E bestow all the blessings we could ask for upon us.

Breaking it down a little more, energy affects other energy through its direction, and we have the choice when it comes to directing the energy. We direct with our feelings, our focus, and our thoughts.

The Big E can't to do it *for* us because The Big E *is* us – expressing through us, *as* us, with us. So the direction is up to us!

As Gandhi said, "Be the change you wish to see in the world." Create the change you wish to experience by choosing, directing, loving, and above all, allowing.

"Ignorance Is Bliss."

There's a wonderful story about some researchers that were compiling stories and information about gnomes and fairies. They decided to visit the elders in the backwood glens of Scotland. Sitting with the eldest of the leaders, they asked him if he remembered ever really seeing a gnome or fairy. "Oh yes," he replied in his thick Scottish brogue. "The gnomes and the fairies used to visit all the time." Stunned, the researcher asked him why they didn't visit anymore. "Oh," he replied, "Then the books came."

In the subjects of creation and manifestation, book learning and mental reasoning can hinder us. Imagination and allowing universal magic to unfold are the secrets to creation.

When we move out of our creativity, we move out of the care of creation. The mind's job is to look for ways to protect us and limit us by keeping us safe. When we realize we can use the mind only as a servant to our own creativity, it can be a useful tool. But a mind without the gnomes and fairies of all possibilities limits joyful creation.

Ignorance is bliss because we are as little children, playing in the never, never land of our own imaginations. Remember when it was okay to be Peter Pan?

"You Don't Know What You've Got 'Till It's Gone."

I can credit the rock band Cinderella with introducing me to this notion. I was in the second grade when their hit single "Don't Know What You've Got, Till It's Gone" was tearing up my Walkman. The idea behind this phrase is that, well, we don't know what we've got until it's gone.

Now, I understand the intention. The implication is to love what you've got while you've got it – because you're really going to miss it when it goes (and it always goes). The danger in buying into this idea is that, once again, according to the law of attraction, what we focus on will appear. If I am focused on having to lose something in order to know its value, guess what? I'm going to create losing it so I can appreciate it. I will create the disappearance of the things I love, so that I can know the value of what I had.

I'd rather know the value of what I have now – while I have it.

If something you love leaves, wish it well and look ahead to your next creation. Dwelling on the past won't help. You can't create in the past. The only place you can create is in this moment. Step back into the present, and create a solution. Create something new to love and appreciate while you are loving and appreciating everything you already are and everything you already have.

"When You Lie Down With Dogs, You Get Up With Fleas."

It's easy to be a monk when you live in a cave. It's just you and your cave (and possibly tivo). You are isolated, and the only person you have to deal with is you. Lying down with dogs is the equivalent of casting your pearls before swine. Pigs aren't going to appreciate your pearls. They're just going to root them further into the mud.

When you lie down with dogs you wake up with fleas because, well, dogs have fleas. It's that simple. You don't have to save anyone, and there are no brownie points for maintaining a high vibration in the face of lower vibrations – other than those you give yourself. Energetic martyrdom is still martyrdom.

It is easier to stay in joy around joyous people than it is to stay in joy around people who hate joy. If you surround yourself with negative people who are always complaining, you may find yourself lowering your vibration rather than raising theirs.

Another way of looking at this is to say that when you hate, you lie down with dogs. When you judge, you lie down with dogs. Any time you move out of love and into fear, you are lying down with dogs. When you move into these vibrations, you push love away. You push your creation away – and what could itch worse than that?

"He Who Lives By The Sword, Dies By The Sword."

"Like attracts like."

"What you see is what you get."

"What goes around comes around."

All of the above nuggets of wisdom (mmm... nuggets. Anyone else in the mood for chicken?) are variances on the title proverb.

When you live in the vibrations of anger and retaliation, you will see the world through that perspective. That perspective will make you focus on those things in your world and draw more anger and retaliation into your consciousness. That triggers more of that vibration in you which puts you into *Re*action. And when we're in reaction, we move out of creation: out of the moment of *choice*.

If someone slaps you and you react, you slap them back and then *they re*act and slap you back. Energetically, no one chooses to NOT REACT and create an opposite vibration of love. He who lives by the slap, dies by the slap. Slower and less painful than the sword, maybe, but the same angry vibration that keeps you out of loving and creating for yourself in a happy, slap-free world.

If we want to die in the same internal world of revenge we are living in, we keep picking up the sword and raising our hand. It's not about whether THEY do, but whether we choose to play or not.

Walk away. Pick up love and abundance and health instead. And bless those that slap their way through life. They know not what they do.

"Good Fences Make Good Neighbors."

This is a true statement... *if* I don't like my neighbors.

So, what is the fear here?

Well, underlying this little ditty are the beliefs of separation and individualism. "Don't let them know too much or they'll spill the beans about who you *really* are." And "keep them at arm's length so they won't ask too much of you." I mean, without that fence, those buggars will be over here borrowing sugar every day!

Basically, if we keep ourselves fenced in, we literally and figuratively keep ourselves from having to experience who we really are. It is through interaction in our relationships that we come to know ourselves best, and see the fears, judgments and limitations of our beliefs.

I say tear all the fences down! I want to experience all my small minded beliefs so I can be free. If I have to fence anything out, I am only fencing myself in. And please...don't fence me in.

"A Merry Heart Makes A Long Life."

Even if that long life is five days.

Initially, I'm sure the meaning behind this is, "The happier you are, the longer you live." And the basis of that has been proven. Love, gratitude and happiness lessen stress which is the root cause of many of our major illnesses today, i.e. heart attack and stroke. Love, gratitude and happiness are also polar opposites of depression, sadness and anger, all of which make life a lot less...merry.

So ultimately, no matter what the actual *time* length ends up being, we live longer lives simply from being in the moment and appreciating it. All those great moments end up being a life of joy and satisfaction – a long, happy life.

No doubt there is a reader perusing this and thinking of a "long life of desperation and suffering." Well, it really isn't the length, but the quality. A long life of hardship is a perspective of life I choose to let go of. A long life of joyful challenges I can (and will) live with. Change your perspective and change your life.

"Let Sleeping Dogs Lie."

You know why? Sleeping dogs don't bite.

We let sleeping dogs lie because no good comes from waking them. If an issue in your life is settled, revisiting it is another way of focusing on it. As long as your attention is on it, you can't move on. If you're not moving on and living in the "now," you can't create anything new. You will continue living in a cycle of re-creation.

The sleeping dog represents a part of your story – past deeds, actions, feelings, beliefs, relationships, etc. By letting the sleeping dog lie, you are saying, "I am willing to give up that part of my story. I no longer need to define myself in that way. I do not need to revisit this subject. I release you."

Letting go of your story is the metaphorical equivalent of being a bad dog owner, because when you can let go, you can release the event from your focus. When your focus has shifted, you are no longer creating being reminded of the problem. In a sense, you forget there was a dog there in the first place. Plus, in the immortal words of *Saturday Night Live's* Bryan Fellows, "I don't wanna get bitt-en!"

"A Good Beginning Makes A Good Ending."

Yes! Intention is everything! *Why* you do something carries throughout your entire creation. And the feeling/vibration that you do it with is the seed that the plant grows from.

Do we begin our creation from love or fear? Desperation or fun? Knowing or hoping? Is it just for the money? Or maybe subconsciously to prove we can't make money!?

And then there is always that annoying little middle part where the intention *can* change. You know – too many hours, too much investment, too many people making you doubt yourself: it can get a person down and lower those initial happy seedlings. And then we JUST WANT TO GET IT DONE, DARN IT! The intention changes, the vibration lowers, and the good ending starts looking farther and farther away.

But wait! We can save that final outcome. We can be conscious! We can choose to find that excitement and passion we had "in the beginning." We can choose to be more balanced so we can stay in love with ourselves and our idea. We can choose NOT to share it with people who don't get it and celebrate it with those who do!

Choose to hold on to yourself love – beginning, middle and end. That's the best ingredient for every intention.

"A Fool And His Money Are Soon Parted."

Well...not if you're Forrest Gump! Forrest loved life. He cared about people. Life was just a box of chocolates. Sweet.

And Forrest made it successfully through his life.

Then there are those people who have really high IQs, lots of "book learning" and degrees and just don't seem to be making it anyway.

So I guess we should look at the definition of "fool." According to the Webster Dictionary, it's "a person lacking in judgment" or "one who is victimized." Guess they don't know either.

Unless, of course, we apply these to Self. If we are lacking judgment ABOUT ourselves and being victimized BY ourselves, then we are sending off messages to the universe that we are ripe for the picking! "Come take my money, my home, my career – because I don't create me. Circumstances create me."

A fool will be parted from anything of value because he doesn't value HIMSELF. And that belief shows up as his life mirrored back to him in his reality. So love yourself – and hold on to your worth!

"Judge Not, Lest Ye Be Judged."

The purpose of this life is to feel good. How many of us feel good with someone yelling in our ear all the time?

"You're not doing it right. Do it this way!"

I was ready to file for divorce half way through that last sentence. The problem is, I can't divorce myself, and that's exactly who my judgment ultimately effects.

You see, when we judge others, we are looking out at the Big E from a limited perspective. What we react to in others is usually what we don't understand about ourselves, what we deny about ourselves, or what we have suppressed deep down within ourselves. When we move into judgment, we move into rejection of an energy that is part of who we are. After all, we *are* all one, and when we judge someone else, we are energetically judging our Self (The Big E).

I'll show you a bit of what I'm talking about here.

Let's pretend I think red headed people are unattractive. I have made a judgment seemingly based simply on my preference for people who do not have red hair – no big deal, right? Well, one day, I meet someone who I find incredibly attractive. I start to approach them, and I get shot down right out of the gate.

"Sorry," they say. "I don't like brunettes."

Huh?! I didn't even get a chance. What's that about?

I'll tell you. The Big E was looking down going, "Hey dude. I see your lips moving, but all I'm able to get from here is sweeping generalizations and judgment." I guess I'll just send you some of that.

Remember, we create what we focus on. So, not only do we create more judgment from judgment, but we also create the situations wherein the actions we are judging can occur. In other words, judge not so you don't limit creation.

"Out of the Frying Pan and Into the Fryer."

In other words: from bad to worse. And you know why? Because while you were in the frying pan, you started focusing on how much you didn't want to be there. You were focused on how terrible things were while being focused on wanting to move. Well, the big E got your call and sent you right over to the fryer.

You see, the big E doesn't judge. If your E is focused on frying, the big E reads ya loud and clear and says, "Okay, more frying!" If you are focused on moving AND focused on frying, you're creating moving into more frying.

The way to hop out of the grease all together is to shoot the big E an instant message and tell it you'd like to move – not because you are having a bad time, but because you want to have a new and joyous experience.

This is the part of the story where I would normally offer a refresher on the law of attraction and how important it is to be in a positive vibration, but by now you've probably heard it a few dozen times. Besides, I'm hungry. All this talk of frying has got me in the mood for bacon.

"Actions Speak Louder Than Words."

Oh – there is so much confusion over this one in the New Age Exploration.

Can't I just sit at a table and have my vibrations attract to me what I want?

Yes.

But the point is: when you are loving yourself, and what you do, you *Want* to take action! Creatively is the SOURCE of manifestation.

So basically, this parable is right. Talk can be pretty cheap. When you actually are living in the vibrations of divine love and excitement and creativity, you HAVE TO MOVE because you are passionately involved in life. When your words are just blah, blah, blahing what you think you should say or the victimness you want to get out of, then the words are hollow, meaningless, and well... cheap. Anyone can read the words from a script. It's a whole other thing to produce it and perform it!

I say we embrace everything we love and take action so the whole world knows it. Then we don't have to talk about it. Like Nike says, "Just Do It."

"The Grass Is Always Greener On The Other Side Of The Fence."

With this belief, you're never truly happy. End of story. Of course, this story assumes that you like green grass.

This belief keeps you always looking somewhere else, focused on what you "want but don't have" which equals being focused on what you don't have which creates more of not having it. No green grass.

We are pressured into always climbing up another rung on that ladder: more success is better, a bigger house is better, more money is better. It's all – greener – when you get there!

If you're not loving the process – or at least lovingly engaging the process (which ultimately means loving yourself) – the chances are, you won't get there anyway. Jealousy, envy, judgment, compromise, etc. will vibrationally take so much fun out of it that the darn fence keeping you from all that green grass might even get bigger. Your grass may start looking really drab.

When you can love creating AND receiving, you are in a harmonious balance with The Big E. Live in gratitude for *now*; be excited in what you're creating *now*, and it is likely the two fields will merge into one great, green pasture of love.

"Don't Make A Mountain Out of a Molehill."

If everyone had ignored the plant in the play *Little Shop of Horrors* it would have died. Instead, they fed it, and everyone ELSE died!

So often in life we keep thinking about what we *don't* want to happen, where we *don't* want to go, the money we *don't* have, the weight we *don't* want and...well, you get the picture. All that focus on the don'ts makes more of the don'ts that we – don't want. We keep feeding the very animal we wish to get rid of. We keep looking at the negative (the "don't") to create the positive (the "please do").

Nine out of ten times when you ask a person what he wants in his life he will tell you all the litany of things he *doesn't* want. And we keep wondering why we aren't creating our desires.

So the next time you find a molehill in your life, say hi to the furry little sucker and move along. Walk around it, step over it, learn the mole lesson if there is one to be had. And then MOVE ON to where you WANT TO BE!!

If you stay stuck at that pesky little molehill, sooner or later it's going to LOOK like the mountain it isn't.

"Don't Sweat The Small Stuff."

My mother used to tell me to only worry about the big stuff: the stuff that deserved worrying! What she didn't know was that worry made the big stuff bigger.

First of all, worry is just a useless expense of energy. Worry doesn't *DO* anything. It just *affects* everything in a lower vibrational oppressive way. Our moods get cranky and impatient; we go out of balance and begin to expect the worst. Not much joyful creation going on with worry.

And of course, worry keeps us focused again on the THING WE DON'T WANT, so the thing seems to grow in intensity and importance and FEAR.

So I say, let's not sweat the big stuff OR the small stuff, because if we sweat the small stuff, it becomes the big stuff and we're back at square one – trying to change our perspective again and focus on what we want. Let's don't sweat anything. Let's glisten with possibilities.

"The Only Thing We Have To Fear Is Fear Itself."

We could use this for day one and just reference it daily for the remaining year.

This one goes all the way back to Sir Francis Bacon (Thanks, internet; I thought it was Teddy Roosevelt!).

When we're in fear, we are immobilized to some degree. It's impossible to be at the zero point of balance, creation and choice because you are in Reaction. Fear makes you want to run/hide/quit/lie/cheat/steal/and fall out of integrity. It puts you into fight or flight, and out of trust.

It's impossible to hold the vibration of fear and love simultaneously. One is a frantic vibration, the other is peaceful calm.

When we are in fear of anything, it owns us. We live in expectation of what "it" will do and what will happen to us.

When we're in love, we create from strength and focus. We are able to see the whole picture from a place of detachment.

Fear Not. Create All.

"Pretty Is As Pretty Does."

I think I heard this every day of my childhood. I never did know what it meant. I just knew it was usually some kind of admonishment regarding an undesirable behavior.

Now, I really get it. My mother was trying to convey to me that if my "vibration" wasn't pretty (i.e. happy, respectful, loving) then *I* wasn't going to be perceived as pretty – no matter how beautiful I appeared.

I experienced this on a whole new level during my first trip to France. I remember thinking, "What is it about the women here, in their plain cotton dresses with no make-up on, that makes them seem so pretty?"

It was simply their aura, their energy, their vibration. They *knew* they were beautiful – and everyone else followed their knowing. It sounds odd, but they literally *reeked* pretty.

Even though Mom's *intention* may have been to use this as a corrective admonishment, she knew what she was talking about. The frequencies you "put out" are the frequencies people receive. They are the most palpable information about you. What you send is what they get. In the same manner, your thoughts and feelings are what The Big E picks up on, and it is according to those thoughts and beliefs, that the universe delivers things unto you. So get pretty!

"Money Doesn't Grow On Trees."

No, but it is made from them.

What's the fear here? Can you see it? Money is a pretty touchy subject to some people, so let me rephrase this one:

"I don't have enough, and even if I did, I would have to horde it because it is hard to come by and there is not enough."

"What? That's not what I said?"

Aw, but it is.

I remember this one really well. My parents were incredibly generous when I was growing up, but there was always a point of stoppage. Specifically, Optimus Prime was a little too expensive for a seven year old who'd already had his birthday.

I wanted that thing so bad. I remember trying to collect money from every member of my family. When my dad heard what I was doing, he chuckled and with the best of intentions said, "Son, Money doesn't grow on trees."

Of course, right after he said that he whipped out his wallet and made me the happiest kid in second grade – but the point is, money is just energy. We often times treat it with such fear and reverence, that we impede its flow into our lives. We think, "You know what? It doesn't grow on trees. I'd better get mine before we run out!" or "I'd better hang on to what I've got!"

Long before our current currency system, civilizations thrived using the barter system. That's all money is. Yes, it is the physical return from a physical investment, but it is also the energetic return from your energetic vibrations.

Choose to vibrate in abundance and look at money for what it really is: a physical manifestation of energy. In other words, money doesn't grow on trees, it grows from you!

"When It Rains, It Pours."

I often hear this statement with regard to unwanted situations. I'll ask someone how their day is going, and they'll proceed to tell me that they broke their foot getting out of the shower the other day, and then they wrecked their car because they got their cast stuck on the peddle, and their insurance just ran out because.... When it rains, it pours.

In truth, this could be used as a positive message as well. Someone could just as easily use it with regard to getting a new job, buying a new house, and falling in love. The perspective may be different, but the same law is at play. That law is the law of attraction: What you focus on appears.

If I am focused on rain, guess what? More and more rain is going to fall. If I am focused on debt, I'm going to get more and more opportunities to create debt. However, if I am focused on abundance, I will have the opportunity to be abundant, and the more I stay focused on and appreciate my abundance the more abundance will come – because hey, when it rains, it pours!

"A New Broom Sweeps Clean."

What happens when you try and clean a new mess with an old broom? You wind up bringing the remnants of an old mess into a new one.

We need to look at each moment not as a continuation of the old, but as the beginning of the new. Every moment is the chance to create everything you want.

If you want a glass of orange juice, do you reach for a clean glass, or do you pour your orange juice into a glass half filled with week old milk? That's easy, right? Week old milk probably doesn't taste so good.

Well, guess what? Your past beliefs, judgments, and experiences are all week old milk.

It's important for us to energetically use a new broom every time we clean, because in doing so, we can create from a new and blank page. We can leave yesterday's garbage out and start from scratch – where we can create anything we want.

"Sticks and Stones May Break My Bones..."

Anyone who's ever spent any time on the playground can finish that sentence. "Sticks and stones may break my bones, but words can never hurt me."

The message here is pretty simple:

If you really want to hurt me, bust me upside the head with a stick.

I'm kidding. The real message here is that words can't hurt you because they are just words. They have no power other than the power you give them.

The reminder here is not to let someone else's words get you down. The only person's words that matter are yours.

Don't let someone else's words wound you. Love yourself enough to recognize your worth in all situations.

And don't hit people with sticks. They may hit back with stones.

"There's No Time Like The Present."

You know why? Cause there's just not.

Can you bring me a glass of water five minutes ago?

Nope.

Can I have a drink of water right now, tomorrow?

Nope.

The "present time" is called "present" time because it's where we create. Every moment is a present, and in order to get your presents, you've got to be in the present.

The only time you can do anything is right now. The past is gone. Just let that one go. Whatever is done is done. You have to forgive yourself and love yourself now – in the present. If you want to change an outcome, you have to create a new one now – in the present. If you want a million dollars next year, you have to start saving and working towards that goal now – in the present. You have to create whatever you want now – in the present.

Now is the only moment of creation. You can't un-create something that has happened. You have to learn to let stuff go so you can quit dragging your past into your present – because by dragging it here, you're re-creating it. Bring in that new broom we talked about earlier, and start clean in every moment.

"Absence Makes the Heart Grow Fonder"

Yep. We always want what we don't have. If it's not in our immediate grasp, we have the luxury of thinking "When I do have it. I'll be happier, richer, more peaceful, fulfilled, in love, etc. Our heart yearns for the absence of what we want because it keeps the HOPE alive that things are better *outside of ourselves.*

What if we celebrated who we are, what we had, and whom we were with? The answer is, we'd have a lot more to celebrate, because it's in the moment of now that we create, and when we're happy and fulfilled IN THIS MOMENT, our vibration stays high and happy *while* our wants are joyously met.

Personally, I don't want to have something absent in my life for my heart to love it more. I don't want to NOT have in order to appreciate what I don't have any more anyway. I want to be on the ride with what makes my heart sing, and I want to celebrate every beautiful moment of having it all.

"After A Storm Comes The Calm."

You've got to love nature. It is always seeking to rebalance itself in harmony. And it has worked since – gosh – the beginning of time!

Nature doesn't sit back and judge itself for having a drought, or for endless rainy seasons any more than it judges itself for the beautiful rainforest and the stunning Sahara. There is no good or bad: no judgment of right and wrong here, just cycles of rebalance. It is the natural ebb and flow that after a storm – when all the build of pent-up energy is released, that nature rebalances itself with rest.

We would all be free if we could simply hold the intention to consistently rebalance ourselves WITHOUT JUDGMENT: to love ourselves and others enough to know this is the experience of life we have chosen by being on earth. Rain/snow, birth/death, rich/poor, sick/healthy: all those wonderful polarities of a three dimensional world!

When we choose to stay in balance, the storms are less severe and pass quickly and the calm remains a lot longer.

"A Guilty Conscience Needs No Accuser."

Nope. We do it all by ourselves. Our internal dialogue goes into a consistent diatribe of judgment, anguish, retribution and self-loathing. Our energy becomes depleted, our vibrations plummet, and we become angry and depressed. We forget that we would probably forgive anyone else but can't be so grandiose as to forgive ourselves.

So much for loving our self!

Again, we are all on this journey of experience. When we call everything on the journey "good," when we know it's all a part of the learning curves, we get to cut ourselves some slack.

Judge not is best applied to self.

Forgive all is best applied to self. Guilty vibrations and love vibrations are an oxymoron: they simply can't live together. They cancel each other out.

If you are holding guilt, take whatever steps you can to rectify it and forgive yourself. If you can't make it right, forgive yourself anyway. It doesn't serve you. It doesn't serve them. And it doesn't serve the world.

You end up falling out of self-creation because you become a victim to your own self judgment. Forgive and forget.

Love makes the world go round.

All you need is love.

Love heals everything.

...'Nuff said.

About the Authors

Jarrad Hewett is a spiritual author who seeks to empower others by sharing his personal humor and insight. Through his writing, he seeks to help others reconnect with their own inner guidance, wisdom, and peace.

For more information, please visit
http://www.jarradhewett.com

Originally from Kansas City, Kansas, *Dee Wallace* is a proud graduate from the University of Kansas where she received her B.A. in Education and Theatre. As an actress, her thirty years of movie magic have touched countless lives.

Having more than 100 television and film credits to her name, Dee has collaborated with some of the most brilliant minds in the industry, including Steven Spielberg, Peter Jackson, Wes Craven, and Stephen King. Her many film credits include such classics as 10, The Hills Have Eyes, The Howling, Cujo, The Frighteners, and most notably her starring role in one of America's most celebrated films, E.T. The Extra-Terrestrial.

Dee is a talented actress, clairaudient healer, and a much sought after motivational speaker who currently hosts the incredibly popular "Conscious Creation Radio" on 7th Wave Network as well as her own weekly segment on the internationally acclaimed Healing With the Masters.

For more information, please visit
http://www.iamdeewallace.com